Monique

May the Peace of
God be with you
always

No More Cursing

DESTROYING THE ROOTS OF RELIGIOUS RACISM

No More Cursing

DESTROYING THE ROOTS OF RELIGIOUS RACISM

Written by

Talbert W. Swan, II, Th.M.

Trumpet in Zion Publishing

Indian Orchard, MA

NO MORE CURSING

DESTROYING THE ROOTS OF RELIGIOUS RACISM

For information:

Trumpet in Zion Publishing
P.O. Box 51163
Indian Orchard, MA 01151

Web site: www.tzpublishing.com

Library of Congress Control Number: 2002096320

ISBN 0 – 9716355 – 1 – X

Printed in the U.S. A.

DEDICATION

To My Son
Talbert W. Swan, III

You are a blessed young man. Always remember that you can do all things through Jesus Christ, who is your strength. I am so proud of you and I know that I am blessed to have you in my life. You are my hero.

Trumpet in Zion Publishing
Indian Orchard, MA

CONTENTS

Preface   i

Introduction   1

1. The Need for the Black Church   9

2. Will the Real Jesus Please Stand Up?   22

3. No Respecter of Persons   34

4. The Myth of Black Inferiority   41

5. Lessons from Samaria   48

6. The Curse of Ham   56

7. Confronting Racism in Religion   76

8. Conclusion   110

End Notes   117

Preface

At the outset of the twenty-first century it appears that the attitude of most white Americans toward black people has changed very little over the years. While many boast of "having black friends" and resent the word "racist" being applied to their thoughts or actions, they are unwilling to take a stance against blatant acts of racism. When Abner Louima was sodomized and brutally beaten by New York police many whites assumed that "he must have done something wrong." When Rodney King was beaten mercilessly by white policemen in front of the entire world, few whites expressed outrage when an all-white jury acquitted the policemen. Over and over again, incidents like these continue to prove that America has made little progress in the area of race relations.

As white America continues to be silent on the issue of race, black leaders continue to rise to oppose this ungodly evil. Yet, every time a black leader addresses issues of race that are systemic in American society he is labeled as being "controversial", a "rabble-rouser", or a "trouble-maker."

Rabble-rousers who threaten the status quo are often attacked by the powers that be in order to discredit them and silence their voice

Jesus was a rabble-rouser. He threatened the status quo and challenged the system in his day. He was such a troublemaker that they had to crucify him to silence his witness.

Rabble-rousers stir the conscious, point out contradictions and declare truth, even when it is not popular to do so. The author of this book is a "rabble-rouser." He, like most African American men in America, has first hand experience with the effects of racism and discrimination. His awareness of religious racism was heightened through theological education and increased interaction with different religious groups. The author has gained a keen awareness of religious racism, particularly in the Christian Church. His most recent endeavors have been attempts to inspire fellow Christians to honestly deal with the subject of racism.

Although the author became involved in civil rights issues on a local level around 1990, it was in 1995, after a White city policeman made a racist telephone call to his church, that he gained public exposure for his efforts to combat discrimination. Ironically, the racist telephone call was in response to a church service the author sponsored to raise funds for black churches in the South that had been burned.

Since receiving the racist telephone call, the author, his family, and his church have been threatened by the "Aryan" brotherhood, harassed by police officers on numerous occasions, and threatened by a fax sent by the police department. The police department investigated the fax incident and alleged that the author sent the fax to himself and falsely accused the department. The District Attorney even convened a grand jury in an attempt to force the author to publicly apologize under the threat of being indicted for filing a false police report. The author refused such an offer and no indictment was ever made.

The sustained efforts of the author to combat racism within his city have gained him plenty of enemies.

However, the belief that God has ordained his social justice ministry has given him the strength and stamina to stay the course regardless of the opposition. A local newspaper once stated, "If Springfield has moved one inch towards rectifying its racial problems in the past year, it is fair to say a full three quarters of that inch is the result of sustained efforts by the Rev. Talbert Swan, II, head of the Solid Rock Church of God in Christ..." (Valley Advocate, Best of Springfield 1997). Several years later, the same paper wrote in an article entitled "26 Pols You Should Know: A roster of the rogues, the righteous and the rabble-rousers who shape Valley politics": "From police brutality to ward representation, Swan stands tough on issues that make more timid types turn and run. Lots of people claim to be leaders in Springfield's African American community, but few have been as consistent and fearless as Swan."

In their 2002 "Who's Who (and What's What) in the Valley", the Valley Advocate wrote the following: "Swan is hated by many in Springfield's political establishment for all the right reasons -- he's smart, unflinching and isn't afraid to call a bigot a bigot, a fraud a fraud and a liar a liar."

After years of addressing the issues of racial discrimination in the broader context of society, the author began to focus on bringing attention to the race problem within the Christian Church. In 1996 an article he wrote on the subject was published in the Springfield Union News' "From the Pulpit" column on the Saturday religious page. Many white clergymen were offended by the article and called the newspaper to voice their displeasure. Based on this outcry, the newspaper made a decision not to use articles written by local clergy. As of the date of this writing the author's 1996 column was the last one published by a local cleric.

Fortunately, not everyone took offense to the article. Shortly after publication of the column, a white Presbyterian pastor named Frederick Porter wrote a letter to the author expressing both his gratitude for the candor in the article and a desire to confront the issue of racial prejudice within himself. Three years later the author and Rev. Porter established the Springfield Christian Leadership Council (SCLC), a group of clergy and lay leaders from throughout the region committed to addressing issues of racism in the Christian community.

The author's life experience, activism within the community, and research on the subject of racial discrimination, compelled him to write this book in order to address a vile untruth that continues to be passed off as an accurate interpretation of the Sacred Scriptures.

It is shameful that in the 21st Century so-called Christians are still teaching the racist doctrine that God cursed African Americans with black skin and ordained the institution of slavery based on an erroneous interpretation of Scripture. The errant "curse of Ham" has been the basis for the mistreatment of black people all over the world. This book addresses this false doctrine and other issues that seem to keep the flame of racism burning brightly within both Christendom and American society as a whole.

INTRODUCTION

The topic of race relations within a Christian context has often brought more controversy than enlightenment. The Christian Church is, by its very essence, composed of "every creature" from "all nations." The Scriptures affirm that God is color-blind and that in Christ physical distinctions do not exist.

Unfortunately, those who claim to follow Christ have not always lived up to His teachings. In some aspects progress has been made in bringing to life the ideals stated in the Gospel, however, more often than not, the church has failed to be a light in a dark world, leading the way to peace and harmony in Christ. The church has not focused its efforts toward breaking down prejudice and dissolving barriers. Even Christians who claim to have no racial bias have been slow to act, thus allowing the world to set the pace toward racial harmony and then following with great caution.

No More Cursing

While the Bible teaches the acceptance and equality of men regardless of race, the Christian Church, which should be leading the way down that road, resists change and continues to disobey God through prejudice and respect of persons. This disobedience has opened the door for religious racists to misinterpret the Holy Writ and claim that racial prejudice is ordained by God and supported by the Scriptures.

Contrary to the felonious exegesis of these pious bigots, the Bible gives no "scriptural" basis for slavery, oppression, or racial prejudice. The two main texts used by these charlatans are Genesis 4:10-15, when God places a mark on Cain after he killed his brother Abel, and Genesis 9:22-27; where Noah is angry with his son Ham and decrees a curse on Ham's son, Canaan. The "mark of Cain" was for his protection, not a punishment. There is no indication that it involved a change in his skin pigment. The so-called "curse of Ham", which was actually on his son Canaan, was fulfilled in the slavery of Canaan's descendants, the Canaanites and has nothing to do with the treatment of Africans in America.

The challenge for the Christian Church is whether its members will be governed by American culture, which is determined by godless and self-serving people or by their Lord and Savior Jesus Christ and what he taught as the standard of human attitude and behavior.

The racist teaching that black skin is a curse and that God ordained the slavery and continued oppression of black people is still being taught in the 21st

Century. Through the years teachers, preachers, and scholars who have reinforced the concept that African Americans are inferior and destined to live a life of oppression and servitude have influenced Christian thought and attitude. Here are some of the vilest viewpoints on race held by so-called Christian leaders:

FINIS JENNINGS DAKE
DAKE'S ANNOTATED REFERENCE BIBLE

For thirty-five years, from 1963 to 1998 this work contained notes in which Dake gave "30 reasons for the separation of the races" where he misuses the Scripture in a demonic attempt to justify his bigotry. He teaches that "God wills the races to be as He made them," and "God made everything to reproduce 'after his own kind,'" applying this to different races.

Contrary to Dake's misguided exposition, the Bible teaches that the "one blood" of Acts 17:26 proves that there is only one race, the human race, and that skin color is only ethnicity.

After much pressure, Dake Publishing omitted some of their racist comments and produced a new Bible in 1998. After hearing that well-known pastor Dr. Frederick K.C. Price was going to devote 30 weeks on Dake's comments in a series he was teaching on racism in the church, the Dake family wrote him a letter apologizing for any offense and asking him not to go forward with the lectures. Dr. Price refused to cancel his lectures and Dake Publishing released a position paper entitled "Answering the Charge of Racism" in which they gave less than compelling evidence that Dr. Dake's commentary was not racist.

Furthermore, the newly published bible simply changed their notes from "30 Reasons for the Separation of the Races" to "Separation in Scripture." All of the reasons listed in the older version have been maintained in the new.

CYRUS INGERSON SCOFIELD
SCOFIELD REFERENCE BIBLE

In 1917, Scofield, a highly influential Bible commentator, wrote in the notes of his reference bible: "A prophetic declaration is made that from Ham will descend an inferior and servile posterity."

BOB JONES UNIVERSITY – SOUTH CAROLINA

This Christian Bible College, in accordance with its so-called opposition to a one-world religion, economic system or political system maintained a long-standing rule against interracial dating. In an apparent strategy to gain the racist vote, Presidential candidate George W. Bush decided to give a speech at this university while on the campaign trail in 2000. In defense of the racist ideology of Bob Jones University, David Lovegrove states the following on his web site"

"BJU stands against a one-world view, which is very Biblical. BJU is opposed to a one-world religion, one-world economic system, or a one-world political system, because these are tools of a system contrary to God. In opposition to those concepts, Bob Jones University created a number of rules to help their students understand the concepts involved. One of those rules was against inter-racial dating. It was not a "black student vs. white student" issue, for blacks

4

were not even allowed as students at the time the rule was made: the rule was put into effect after a situation arose with a white and an Asian. Dr. Jones stated that the rule was an insignificant part of BJU - so insignificant, he said, that it had not been preached on in chapel or taught in a class for four or five generations of students - fifteen or twenty years"

Neither Mr. Lovegrove nor Bob Jones University has been able to explain what interracial dating has to do with the college's opposition to a one-world system.

MATTHEW HALE, FOUNDER WORLD CHURCH OF THE CREATOR

Matthew Hale admits that he is a racist. In 2000 he stood before an audience of 1000 at the historic 16th Street Baptist Church in Birmingham Alabama where four little black girls were killed in a racist bombing in 1963. He was a participant in a Newsweek/MSNBS town hall meeting called "Shades of Progress...Shadows of Hate." Standing opposite civil rights leader Rev. Al Sharpton, Hale declared that white people don't want a diverse, multi-cultural America. "They want a white community for themselves, not an integrated cesspool.", he said.

Hale's so-called "church" holds to a Christianized white supremacy ideology. Benjamin Smith, one of Hale's followers, killed Ricky Byrdsong, an African-American, in Chicago in 1999.

These are just a few examples of current and past "Christian" teaching that has permeated our society and influenced the thinking and actions of many throughout the history of this country. Although these doctrines have no biblical basis they have been promulgated as truth.

Because those who have espoused these nefarious contentions are labeled as Christian leaders makes them no better than any other white supremist. They are on the same level as the Skinheads or the Ku Klux Klan. Sadly, their station in life has allowed them to have great impact and given them credibility in the Christian community. We still live in a day and age where your average Christian assumes that if something is written in the notes of a Bible or espoused from the pulpit it must be rooted in truth. This has sadly led to many whites, even those who won't verbalize it, holding the notion that Black people are indeed, inferior.

The church has failed in the fight against racism by both its participation in and complicity towards acts of racism. In his book Race, Religion & Racism, Volume I, Dr. Frederick K.C. Price accurately notes that slavery could have never existed in America without the complicity of the church.

"Christian" bigots have perverted the Bible to justify the mistreatment of Black people. The church has been the main participant in acts of racism throughout history. The enslavement and subsequent oppression and discrimination against Blacks were met with approval from many Christian leaders. They taught that God ordained slavery and twisted the Scripture to promote the lie that Blackness was a curse. The church has not only failed in its responsibility toward its Black brothers and sisters, it has failed God by perpetrating, promoting, condoning, or being complicit about racism.

As a Church of God in Christ (COGIC) minister I am mindful that the roots of my denomination are embedded in the Azusa Street revival in Los Angeles in the early twentieth century. During this historic move of God the Christian Church was given an opportunity to make a statement to the world by unifying believers of every race and culture. A black preacher named William Seymour led this great revival that birthed not only the COGIC but also the Pentecostal movement in America. Sadly, after only a few years, the Assemblies of God and other predominantly white Pentecostal denominations were formed after whites decided to succumb to the climate of racial hate in America.

A friend introduced me to a video on the subject of racism entitled "White Privilege." The very notion that white people have privileges that others don't is a controversial subject with profound implications. The average white person will deny that he or she benefits from privileges that non-whites do not enjoy. This is the typical attitude of many white people who are ignorant of their own racism. The ability to ignore and deny the truth about one's feelings toward race is one of the privileges of being white. This is especially true within the Christian Church. Many of the concerns of non-white Christians can easily be ignored by white Christians and white churches. Those unaffected by discrimination can easily write off claims by non-white people of mistreatment as another incident of "playing the race card." So often I hear my white Christian brothers and sisters rationalize mistreatment of blacks and Latinos with statements like, "they must have done something to deserve it."

Contrary to popular opinion, the scourge of racial prejudice has an affect on the mission of all Christians regardless of race. Discrimination and the lack of response to it by the church hinder effective evangelism and betray the witness of professing Christians. The fact that the white church has been spineless and afraid to speak with a loud effective voice against the sin of racism has produced a culture in Christendom that is similar to that in the world. Sadly, racism is alive and well within the church.

The intent of this book is not to lambaste my fellow Christian brothers and sisters, however, in order to effectively deal with the issue of racism within the church we must engage in frank and honest dialogue. The goal of this book is to present an accurate exegesis of Biblical texts that have been used to promote a doctrine endorsing the enslavement, oppression, and mistreatment of African Americans in the United States of America due to the so-called "curse of Ham." For far too long the white church has espoused and supported this racist doctrine, which teaches that black people are, by God's divine plan, inferior. In order to enlighten those who either teach this erroneous doctrine or have been confused by it, we will seek to prove that, unlike man, God doesn't regard any race superior to another that He has created.

CHAPTER 1
THE NEED FOR THE BLACK CHURCH

The role of the Black Church throughout the history of America has been that of the leading entity in the fight for social justice and civil and human rights. The fact that this institution has not just struggled for African Americans, but for all Americans is profound. The prolonged endeavor of the Black Church in the area of civil rights coupled with its mission to serve the poor and disenfranchised while giving spiritual guidance to its congregants and being the moral conscious of a country that has resisted racial equality is a powerful accomplishment.

It is quite amazing that our African ancestors were taught a form of Christianity that would make them better tools of service for their oppressors, yet adopted a theology of liberation that would not accept "slaves be obedient to your masters" as a directive to remain in bondage. They developed a philosophy that supported the eradication of the racist institution of slavery, which kept them from being free.

THE BIBLE TAUGHT LESSONS OF FREEDOM

Africans like Nat Turner, Harriet Tubman, and Sojourner Truth translated their understandings of the Bible into a justified battle for emancipation against their racist white oppressors. They used the Bible to prove fact that God intended for them to be free. They sang songs like "Go down Moses, way down in Egypt land. Tell ole, Pharaoh, to let my people go." Egypt, of course, represented the American South and Pharaoh represented the white slave master.

Although the Black Church has often been criticized for its focus on a better existence in the after-life and the so-called "pie in the sky" theology, we cannot ignore the fact that it played an active role in the anti-slavery society of antebellum America.

THE STRUGGLE FOR JUSTICE

The training ground for leaders has always been found in the Black Church. Few other institutions were open to up-and-coming leaders of the community. The church was the place where strong activists were made.

The struggle for justice in a nation where the social, political, and economic structures have always been dominated by a white supremacist mentality required an institution that was independent and strong enough to challenge America's racist ideology. The Black Church, seeing beyond white distortions of the

Bible and grasping its true meaning of liberation became the premier institution for the liberation of Black people. The fact that our ancestors believed that God would bring their oppressors to justice gave them the strength to endure the hardships of slavery and the courage to fight against unbeatable odds. Early Black preachers preached about the importance of love. Their theology of love didn't only mean that they should love their enemies, but that God's love for them was linked with His justice. Therefore, hope for liberation endured.

Though they were treated as less than human, slaves believed that God created everyone in His divine image. They understood that all men were created equal long before it was written in America's sacred documents. This inherent equality made each of them sacred. Regardless of what white America said about them, they had an assurance that they were indeed the children of God. White America's violation of their dignity was a direct sin against God's law of love. The Good Book said that we must love our neighbor because God first loved us. Because the institution of slavery violated the dignity of the human personality, God would have to mete out justice because "whatsoever a man sows, that shall he reap."

SEEING BEYOND THE DISTORTIONS

The slaves discovered the great contradiction between what the Bible taught them and how the slave master treated them. They did not allow their mistreatment to keep them from receiving the truth of the Bible. In spite of their horrible circumstances they maintained hope for a brighter tomorrow, courage to confront the atrocities of slavery, and strength to

11

endure the most brutal form of bondage history has ever known. The Biblical truths they found hidden behind the slave master's distortions enabled them to endure hardships that we can only imagine.

The slave's enduring faith inspired generation after generation of leaders to respond courageously to the oppression of Black people. Church inspired leaders were the likes of Gabriel Prosser, Denmark Vessey, and Frederick Douglas. However, the Black church's interpretation of scripture inspired far more than those whose names are most familiar as thousands of former slaves enlisted in the Union Army during the Civil War to fight for the freedom that the Bible promised to every man.

The message of liberation as contained in the Bible caused Southern states to restrict missionary activities among slaves. They forbade reading instruction and limited preaching by slave preachers. They also restricted slave worship services. In his book "The History of the Negro", Carter G. Woodson quotes Bishop Asbury from his 1776 Journal saying, "I met the class and then the black people, some of whose unhappy masters forbid their coming for religious instruction. How will the sons of oppression answer for their conduct when the great proprietor of all shall call them to account?"[1]

Understanding the stark difference between the slave master's version of Christianity and what he actually practiced, the slaves indicted their oppressor's conduct through the lyrics of a song that stated, "Everybody talkin' 'bout Heaven ain't goin' there."

A CHALLENGE TO THEIR FAITH

In spite of their strong faith, their belief in God's justice and their hope for liberation, oppression was not easy. The continuous suffering challenged the faith of the slaves. The age-old question was, if God is good, why would he allow people to be stolen from Africa and enslaved in a strange land? None of us have ever been able to evade the great mystery of that agonizing inquiry.

Even when their faith was challenged, the slaves continued to believe that since God delivered Moses and his people, he would also deliver them. Black identification with the biblical story of Moses and their exodus from Egypt has always been strong. Like Moses, the Black preacher was called to lead his people from America, the modern day Egypt, and from the slave master, the modern day Pharaoh. The symbolism of being led out of Egypt continued beyond slavery and into the civil rights era. In his final speech, a century after emancipation, Dr. Martin Luther King, Jr. reflected "we as a people will get to the Promised Land."

THE MEANING OF "EGYPT"

From the Black Church's perspective, Egypt meant and continues to mean enslavement and captivity. As the only people illegally captured and brought to America to be used for slave labor, the Black experience in America is consistent with this perspective. It is insulting when I read the writings of narrow-minded historians that claim American slavery as the most "humane". The rising of Black churches and civil rights organizations clearly weren't

13

influenced by the "humane" treatment of Blacks during American slavery. It is absolutely necessary for the Black Church and any serious theologian to continue to explore the motif of "Egypt." It is only through this perspective that we can continue to empower the Black Church and facilitate its mission of liberation.

FREEDOM DID NOT BRING EQUALITY

As history records, emancipation from slavery neither made Blacks equal in the eyes of white America nor ended their problems in this country. After reconstruction the systematic and legal oppression of Black people remained intact. Those who claimed to be Christians were at the forefront of the continued efforts to suppress Black people. Of course, this is a major point of contention among white theologians. To this day many white church leaders continue to deny both the current and historical complicity of the white church during the oppression of Black people. The daily newspaper in my city runs a Saturday column on the religion page called "From the Pulpit." I was the featured columnist on several occasions; however, one column in particular stands out. I wrote a column on racism in the church that was published on Saturday, September 7, 1996 that criticized the churches in my city for their intentional silence and refusal to address the social, political, economic, and spiritual concerns of the downtrodden members of the Black community. The column instigated a flurry of calls to the newspaper complaining about its content. Sadly, the newspaper made a decision not to publish columns from local clergy. As of the date of this writing, nearly years after my column was published, all published columns have come from wire services and none have dealt with the church's responsibility in the area of social justice.

White churches in my city today are much like white churches in the South during slavery and segregation. Many either are completely silent about racism or loudly defend the reprehensible conduct of those who oppress Black people. The white church was a major supporter of the Ku Klux Klan and other white supremacist groups that were responsible for the intimidation and lynching of Black people. Most Black families today have stories of relatives or friends who were abused or murdered during the dark days of slavery and segregation or during modern times where police seemingly have a license to kill Black people at will.

THE BLACK CHURCH, A PLACE OF REFUGE

The Black community has always found refuge in the church. When they were denied a decent wage to support their families, abused by authority figures, prohibited from voting, and denied the right to exercise their gifts and talents in favor less talented white folks, Black people have always had their needs met in the church. It was the church that gave people protection from those who would harm them, peace in times of trouble, and comfort and strength in a community that refused to accept their full humanity. The relevance, progression, influence, and power of the Black Church is well documented despite the claim by critics that it has taught Black people to accept oppression in hopes of a better day in the after-life. It cannot be refuted that the Black Church is and has been the essence of the movement to liberate Black people.

After emancipation, it was the Black Church that took on the important task of educating the newly freed slaves. It was in the churches where Black colleges were conceived and given birth to. The church easily became the center of Black life; it was the school, the social center, the meeting place, and the house of worship. Many of the civil rights organizations that came into being had their roots in the church. It was in the church that the National Association for the Advancement of Colored People (NAACP) held its meetings and membership drives. It has always been church leaders that have provided strong leadership for the black community at large.

CHRISTIANITY, A WHITE MAN'S RELIGION?

Critics of the Black Church have often suggested that Christianity has been a white man's religion that has been a pacifying force in the Black community. I never turn down the opportunity to present the evidence that proves that Christianity has always been the major source of comfort, strength and hope for Black people. Faith in Jesus Christ has been the driving force behind activism throughout the history of Black America. Of course, this doesn't dismiss the fact that some of our people have listened to lies and to misinterpretations of biblical passages. This has developed in some an unhealthy view of themselves and Black people in general. However, those who have followed the liberating doctrine of Christianity have been and continue to be effective leaders. An interview with many successful Blacks would reveal that their relationship with Jesus instigated their struggle and was the catalyst to their success.

The fact is, Christianity was one of many African religions and was not introduced to Africans in America. It just so happens that the version of Christianity that has spread throughout Europe and America is a hellenized version. Alexander the Great had a mission to spread Greek culture (hellenize) throughout the world. The tainted version of Christianity that was taught by the slave master was, in part, influenced by the "whitenizing" of Christianity.

Christianity spread throughout Africa and Ethiopia, which was the first "Christian" country. The Christian Coptic Church of Ethiopia, which is over three thousand years old, is the oldest Christian church in the world. As Christianity spread throughout Europe, it mixed with European culture and was defiled by white supremacy, what I call "whitenizing." Because of its whitenizing, Christianity became a tool to promote white supremacy and had little to do with the oppressed and the downtrodden.

During the Slave trade white artists in Europe began to paint pictures of whitenized Biblical characters, including Jesus and His mother Mary. Soon, every prophet and noteworthy person in Biblical history became white. They ignored the book of Revelation's declaration that Jesus had feet like brass and hair like lamb's wool and depicted him with white skin, blue eyes, and blond hair.

Although it is this whitenized version of Christianity that Blacks were exposed to, we cannot ignore the fact that Christianity has always been a part of African life and reduce it to the level of a vile religion based on white supremacy.

LEADERSHIP OF THE BLACK CHURCH

The Black Church has been a place of stability and strength. Ironically, it was the scourge of racism in America that gave Blacks this powerful institution. Because they were prevented from fully participating in the religious institutions of white America, Blacks developed their own churches. These churches empowered participation in politics, music, drama, education, finances, arts, economic and community development, social services, the struggle for civic rights, and business development. When there was no where else to go, Blacks could find spiritual guidance, encouragement, and a doctrine of liberation. It was only in church that Blacks would hear that they were equal to whites and were indeed God's children. This message confirmed that they were not cursed as white Christians had told them for so long. It also gave them assurance that they didn't need to wait until the day "it will all be over" for them to have "no more heartache and no more suffering."

The role the Black Church has played in the development of leadership, the abolishment of slavery, and the struggle for civil rights cannot be matched by any institution. The civil rights struggle in this country was a Black Church movement and a social revolution. It is because of the church that there was a Voting Rights Act and that desegregation took place. Today it is the Black Church that continues to fight for social change in America.

The Black Church has provided a forum that accepts, acknowledges and respects members of the Black community regardless of socio-economic status or educational background. Where else can an uneducated man with a minimum wage paying job go and be head of a deacon board among members that are more educated and are in a higher socio-economic class? The church has become the only place for many in the Black community to go. It is in the church that they are given valued roles, which give them a sense of self worth.

The Black Church has kept people aware of social issues through political messages, rallies, forums, and meetings. The church has always been an entity that has stressed the importance of social and political action.

The Black community's most effective leaders have been taught and nurtured in the "cultural and spiritual womb"[2] of the church. Black Church leaders have preached, taught, and led the community into a transformational spiritual, social, political, economic, and cultural reality. The central role of the Black Church throughout its history has made it the premier institution in Black America.

Blacks have always been spiritual people. When it comes to Christianity, their experience has been transformed from a racist environment dominated by whites that looked on them as inferior to one that has empowered them to move beyond the unfortunate circumstances forced on them by a racist society. Because of the supremacist attitude of white Christians, the Black Church adopted a mission to empower its members, develop their leadership, and restore their dignity.

PERTINENT QUESTIONS

As we move through the beginning of the twenty-first century, the conditions in which we live are structured within the same racist system that has polluted the Black experience in this country. Because of this dynamic, the Black Church is no less relevant today than it was during slavery or segregation. Let's ponder several questions: Are Black people experiencing the exclusionary attitudes and practices that were encountered during slavery and segregation when they attempted to become a part of mainstream churches? Do Black people feel welcomed and embraced in mainstream white churches? Has the white church changed its historical role of remaining silent on issues of racial discrimination? Has America's attitude toward the equality of Black people changed significantly enough for the Black Church to scrap the message of liberation? If we honestly answer these questions in the negative, we must conclude that the Black church's mission of liberation needs to continue. While we must acknowledge the gains that have been made in the area of social justice, we must also be honest about the racist attitudes and practices in America that have remained status quo.

Since the Black Church in America had to separate from mainstream white churches in order to empower its members, develop their leadership, and restore their dignity, it must continue to lead the way to the

"Promised Land", a place that can only be found in true Christian unity.

CHAPTER 2
WILL THE REAL JESUS PLEASE STAND UP?

Over the years, many have labeled Christianity as a "white man's religion" and have held the opinion that the Bible was contaminated by white men and cannot be trusted. While I vehemently disagree with the label of Christianity as a "white man's religion," I can understand the distrust of Christianity within the context of its distortion by white people. The use of the so-called "curse of Ham" to justify 400 years of slavery and the long history of the abuse of Black people at the hands of European Christians has left a bitter taste in the mouths of many.

CHRISTIANITY USED TO OPPRESS

We cannot deny that whites have used Christianity as a tool to oppress non-white people around the world. The white version of Christianity was used to justify the enslavement and exploitation of Black people since Europeans first set foot on the Africa continent. Sadly, they saw no contradiction between their inhumane treatment of Blacks and the biblical teachings they claimed to live by. In America, white men could, in good conscious, lynch a Black man on Saturday and praise the Lord in church on Sunday. They saw their actions as part of God's punishment of Black people for being "heathens." Blacks were told that they would be able to enjoy heaven after they died if they were good slaves on earth. Since Black people were not allowed to read or write it was easy to instill these vicious lies into their psyche. This kind of brainwashing created a form of mental slavery, which was much more dangerous than physical slavery. Mental slavery has had long-lasting effects on Blacks as a people throughout the history of America.

LIES TOLD

Whites taught Blacks that we were swinging on trees when they were stolen from Africa. They stripped them of their history, culture or religion and told them that their affiliation with white people should be considered a blessing. Blacks were robbed of their human dignity by carefully orchestrated lies and tactics designed to keep them in bondage. There are many social problems, which exist today that are a direct result of these lies and tactics.

Racism has long been part of the belief system of the type of Christianity practiced by many whites. This form of Christianity has always sought to provide a rationale to justify racial divisions and to divide and rule society along racial lines. It has supported the idea that biological, hereditary, and cultural differences verify the superiority of white people.

AN ATTITUDE OF SUPERIORITY

This has been the basis for the white church's attitude of superiority and their support of America's right to rule over others. To this day it is difficult for many white Christians to see how this attitude is fundamentally incompatible with what the Bible teaches.

In spite of the glaring contradictions between biblical principles and white Christian behavior, we cannot conclude that Christianity only represents those who would use it to oppress others. The Christianity practiced by Black people and the religion practiced by their oppressors is not within the same sphere.

THE QUESTIONS BEFORE US

The questions now before us are; which type of Christianity is authentic? Is Christianity a white man's religion? and, if there are two types of Christianity, which one does Jesus represent? These are the theological issues raised by the racism that has been practiced and condoned by the white church in America.

Black people have always seen Jesus as one who is on the side of the poor and oppressed. Whites have seen Him as the champion of their causes. While whites view Jesus as one in support of slavery, capitalism and colonialism, Blacks perceive the cross as a symbol of freedom and liberation. For it was "at

24

the cross where I first saw the light and the burdens of my heart rolled away." Whites have seen this same cross as a symbol of power, which has been used to bring the non-white world into subjection.

THEOLOGICAL DIFFERENCES

The sharp theological differences between white and Black versions of Christianity still exist today. The Black Church must continue to preach about a Jesus that will lead His people to freedom and not one who is unconcerned with the social ills that still exist in America. Black Christianity looks for freedom, justice and equality among all people while white Christianity looks forward to a day when no one opposes its power.

At the time of this writing, America was embroiled in a so-called "war on terrorism" in response to the September 11, 2001 attacks on the World Trade Center in New York City and the Pentagon in Washington, D.C. What amazes me is the outpour of support from mainstream white churches for a "war" on an unidentified enemy in an apparent act of retribution. When the seat of capitalism is attacked white churches see it as their patriotic duty to respond. After all, this is "one nation under God", right?

In the 1990's when millions of Blacks in Rwanda were slaughtered, both the American government and the white church were silent. Firm opposition to this genocide could have saved hundreds of thousands of lives, however, international leaders and mainstream Christian churches refused to even speak the word "genocide." They failed to denounce the evil either

25

jointly, or through singular efforts. Throughout the consistent reign of terror on Black men by American police forces across the country, the white church has remained silent. In 1998 when terrorist bombed U.S. embassies in Dar Es Salaam, Tanzania and Nairobi, Kenya and claimed the lives of hundreds of Africans, the white church was also silent.

While I wholeheartedly denounced the vicious attacks on the World Trade Center and the Pentagon, I can't help but wonder why these attacks deserved the support, prayers, and strength of mainstream white churches and others didn't.

The Jesus of Black Christianity would be against terrorism whether or not the victims came from the ranks of mainstream white America. Perhaps the Jesus mainstream white churches follow is the same as the one their forefathers gave their devotion to. It is no wonder some question whether or not Blacks should follow Jesus. However, the more appropriate question is; which Jesus should Black people follow?

CHALLENGING THE EXISTING SOCIAL ORDER

Christina Noble (pseudonym), a scholar on religion in America, characterized the relevance of antebellum Christian faith as follows:

"Christianity in antebellum America merely conformed to prevailing cultural trends. Christians in varied contexts whether slave or free, black or white tailored their faith to fit their respective situations. Their faith neither challenged the existing social order nor reinterpreted their roles in it. The failure of professed

Christians to take a public stand against antebellum oppression compromised the authenticity of their religion."

History will only allow me to agree with one of Ms. Noble's claims. She was accurate in her claim that Christians tailored their faith to fit their respective situations. The slave-owners gave their slaves a form of Christianity that was adapted to fit their purposes. Those who preached to slaves explained that if the slaves were patient on earth they would receive a reward in Heaven. Slave-master Christianity was designed to convince slaves that if he or she was whipped, worked to death, or separated from his or her family, happiness would come in Heaven.

Some slaves believed these explanations; however, most adapted the religion to meet their own ends. The slaves studied the Old Testament and learned about Moses leading the Israelites out of Egypt. They related that story with their plight in the United States.

They also took a special interest in stories about Judgment Day. That would be the day that "massa" would have to stand before God and pay for all of his crimes. A Black preacher named Nat Turner prepared his followers for an uprising by preaching about the Judgment Day. Ms Noble obviously didn't consider the fact that Turner's faith reinterpreted his role in society. This faith also reinterpreted the roles of many slaves in the antebellum South. Their faith dictated that they were no longer someone else's property, destined to live in bondage forever. They were like Israel, and God was going to let white people feel the same pain that was inflicted upon Blacks. Their prayers were not for God to make them better slaves, but to let the judgment fall on their oppressors. Aggy, a slave housekeeper prayed that God would "hasten de day when de blows, an' de bruises, an' de aches, an' de pains shall come to de white folks, an' de buzzards shall eat 'em as dey's dead in de streets." [3]

The role of Black people in the existing social order was justified by Christian slave-owners that said God ordained their plight as slaves. However, the slave's faith in the story of the Exodus "contradicted the claim made by white Christians that God intended Africans to be slaves."[4] The faith of the slave gave new meaning to their lives. That same faith gave Nat Turner a sense of purpose. He was convinced that he was "ordained for some great purpose in the hands of the Almighty"[5]

It was the reinterpretation of his role in the existing social order that caused Turner, contrary to Ms. Noble's claims, to challenge the existing social order. His first challenge to the existing social order was to run away. Turner and many other slaves believed that God had a better place prepared for them, and they were willing to risk their lives to get there. However, Turner was convinced that he was called by God to challenge the existing social order on a higher level than simply running away, thus, after thirty days as a fugitive he returned to his slave-master. In a confession made to his captors, Turner explained that signs in Heaven let him know that he would have to begin a great work by killing his enemies with their own weapons.[6]

On an Early summer morning in 1831, Nat Turner and his followers challenged the existing social order like none before them. Their challenge carried them into history. In his confession to Thomas Gray, Turner explained most of his motives for leading a revolt that killed 55 white people in religious terms. It is evident that he saw his devotion to freedom as part of his faith. It was his faith that caused him to challenge the existing social order to the point that he showed no remorse for his actions. He was convinced that God inspired what he had done.

Perhaps the bloodiest slave insurrection of all time began that early summer morning in Southampton County, Virginia. Turner, its leader, besides being a skilled carpenter, was a literate preacher who had discovered relevance in the prophets of the Old Testament. Besides identifying with the slave experience of the Israelites, Turner was convinced that the social righteousness, which the prophets preached, related directly to the plight of the slaves. The picture of the Lord exercising vengeance against the oppressors gave Turner and his followers hope and inspiration.

While the Bible appeared to tell the slave to be faithful and obedient to his master, it also condemned the wicked and provided examples that proved God's willingness to use human instruments in order to bring justice against oppressors. Turner's hatred of slavery and his concern for the plight of his brothers led him to believe he was one of God's chosen instruments.

As his conviction deepened, the solar eclipse early in 1831 appeared to him to be a sign that the day of vengeance was at hand. In the following months he collected a small band of followers, and in August they went into action. Unlike Gabriel Prosser and

Denmark Vesey, he began with only a very small band, which lessened his chance of betrayal. As they moved from farm to farm, slaughtering the white inhabitants, they were joined by many of the slaves who were freed in the process. However, word of the massacre soon began to spread. At one farm, armed resistance met them. Slaves as well as masters fought fiercely to stop the attack. Some of Turner's men were killed and others were wounded. The planned drive toward the "Promised Land" was thrown off stride. This enabled the militia to arrive and break up the attack. In due time Turner and several of his followers were captured and executed.

White men in both the South and the North saw little similarity between slave insurrections such as this and the American Revolution. The Turner massacre was nearly universally depicted as the work of savages and brutes, not of men. Vigilance was tightened, and new laws controlling the slaves were passed throughout the South. Both the violence of the slaves and the verbal abuse of the abolitionists only served to strengthen the South in its defense of the racist institution of slavery. Slaves who revolted were depicted as beasts that could not be freed because they would endanger society. Submissive slaves were pictured as children in need of paternal protection from the evils of a complex, modern world. They were never seen as men whose rights and liberties had been proclaimed in the Declaration of Independence.

Nat Turner helped to bury the lie that Blacks were happy as slaves and would forever submit to the cruelties of their slave masters. He changed the everyday pattern of whites across the state of Virginia during his time. After his revolt, slave-owners no longer left their doors unlocked. They constantly checked the pistols under their beds and they woke up with every noise. Virginia's peaceful sleep was ended by the actions of a slave preacher acting upon his faith.

WHAT IS AUTHENTIC CHRISTIANITY?

How do we judge the authenticity of Christianity? Many will say that Nat Turner could not have been truly Christian if he felt justified in killing people. Likewise, the Christian slave-master believed he was within his God-given right to rule over the "inferior" African slave that his God had placed him over. Most slaves believed that God would deliver them from their oppression and did nothing, while others thought like Nat Turner and took matters into their own hands, believing that God would be on their side.

Sadly, I don't believe I will live to see the day that one set of standards or facts measures Christianity. The argument over what viewpoint Jesus would support will continue for many years. However, there is one fact that should be constant in Christianity, that all men are equal. Jesus preached the equality of all men throughout his ministry. Therefore, the Jesus of the Bible cannot be the same man that white Christians in this country have followed.

JESUS OF THE MAINSTREAM WHITE CHURCH

The Jesus mainstream white churches continue to follow must be the same one they attempted to force upon the slaves. Karl Marx once said, *"religion is the sigh of the oppressed creature, the heart of a heartless world, and the soul of soulless conditions. It is the opium of the people."* The religion that whites taught the slaves was a religious narcotic given to numb the agony of their pain and suffering in America.

JESUS OF THE BLACK CHURCH

In spite of the attempt to intoxicate Blacks with a religion that would render them passive and make them into obedient tools of service, a different Jesus stood up in their hearts. This Jesus taught from a different perspective than the Jesus that the slave master followed. This Jesus taught that those guilty of oppression would be called to account for their actions. He also taught them that he would set them free and that "he who the Son sets free is free indeed" (John 8:34-36). No matter how much the white preacher told them that slavery was God's will, they refused to give up the idea that Jesus wanted them to be free. They risked everything to practice a religion that would bring about their freedom.

The freedom their Jesus talked about was the kind of freedom the slaves had in spite of their physical shackles. This freedom, found only in their hearts and minds, caused them to rise above their sufferings. This freedom has been the catalyst for the fight for freedom and justice. A relationship with a liberating Jesus gave them hope for the future and power to change their conditions. They were able to move beyond looking for Heaven in the "sweet bye and bye." Heaven not only meant a place to go after life ended, it also became anyplace freedom existed.

Africa, Canada and the northern United States became the "Promised Land."

WILL THE REAL JESUS PLEASE STAND UP?!

The slaves found a Jesus that was a kind, compassionate, and powerful friend. He was a man that so identified with their suffering that he came from Heaven to become one of them. He suffered and died and was resurrected in order to free them of their suffering. The Jesus they knew was the only sure and lasting hope for freedom. Black people were not an afterthought nor were they a cursed people to the Jesus they worshipped and adored. This is the Jesus that the Black Church has taught about down throughout the centuries. Today, many churches are rediscovering this Jesus. Mainstream white theologians have repudiated the preaching of this Black Jesus and the displaying of His picture in churches across America. Many, including Blacks, claim that the color of Jesus doesn't matter and that Christianity is color-blind. Many of us in the Black Church know better.

To every Christian, Black or white, their religion is authentic according to their interpretation of what their faith defines them as in the existing social order. Their religion is also authentic based on their interpretation of who Jesus really is and what he really stands for. Will the real Jesus please stand up!

CHAPTER 3

NO RESPECTER OF PERSONS

What does the Bible say about racial differences, and how should believers approach this question of race and race relations? Misinterpretation of the Bible has led some to believe that God placed a curse upon Black people, making them an inferior race of people. This is based upon an erroneous understanding of the curse placed on Canaan after the Flood, which started with the sin of Noah.

The story of this curse must have taken place years after the flood because Noah's son Ham already had children. Noah had planted a vineyard, got drunk and laid down in a drunken stupor.

When Ham entered Noah's tent and saw his naked father, he told his two brothers. In contrast to Ham's action, his brothers, Shem and Japheth, went into their father's tent backward, so as not to see Noah's condition, and they covered his naked body. When Noah awoke, he inquired what his younger son had done to him. After hearing what Ham had done he pronounced a blessing on Shem and Japheth and a curse, not on Ham, but on one of Ham's four sons, Canaan. Many think that the curse was placed on Ham and thereby on African people. Ham's other sons, Cush - Ethiopia; Mizraim - Egypt; and Phut – Libya populated Africa. However, Canaan was the father of the people in Phoenicia, Palestine, and Canaan.

Contrary to what some teach, God is not concerned with race. His message of salvation through faith in Christ is for all men, regardless of ethnic background. God's judgments and blessings are without partiality.

The concept of *"race"* is biological, not Biblical. There is no mention of different races, as defined in modern times, in the Bible. Evidently, there is no Biblical or theological meaning to the term, and we must conclude, therefore, that races are purely arbitrary entities invented by man for his own convenience in biological and anthropological studies.

All races are a part of the human race. We have made the term race apply to skin color; however, race really refers to individuals with common characteristics, interests, appearances, or habits as if derived from a common ancestor.

Skin color is essentially a biological difference that has caused a struggle between races. All men who have ever lived in the world are descendants of Adam and, therefore, are of the same race, the human race. Act 17:26 states: "God hath made of one blood all nations of men for to dwell on all the face of the earth"

No More Cursing

USING THE BIBLE TO
JUSTIFY RACIAL PREJUDICE

Regardless of its obvious contradiction to the doctrine of racial prejudice, the Bible continues to be used to justify racial prejudices. Scripture passages forbidding Israel to mingle with their enemies are used to infer that God is against intermarrying. In actuality, the concern expressed in these passages was that Israel not be influenced to indulge in pagan worship. Yet, the bigots continue to ignore the fact that the Scripture clearly teaches against respect of persons based on race. Consider the following Scriptures:

"My brothers have not the faith of our Lord Jesus Christ with respect of persons." (James. 2:1); "It is not good to have respect of persons in judgment." (Deuteronomy. 1:17); "There is no respect of persons with God." (Romans. 2:11); "No respect of persons with him." (Ephesians. 6:9); "God is no respecter of persons." (Acts 10:34); "And there is no respect of persons." (Colossians. 3:25); and "God judges without respect of persons." (I Peter. 1:17).

Blinded by his or her own hatred and supremacist attitude, the religious racist chooses to ignore the clarity of God's will on the subject of race. The deliberate respect of persons based on race is a sin that the Christian Church is obligated to speak against.

PREJUDICE IN THE CHURCH DATES
BACK TO THE DAYS OF THE APOSTLES

The Apostle Peter once said, "It is unlawful for a Jew

to keep company with other nations." He soon had a change of heart after God gave him a vision and released him to preach to the Gentiles. After preaching to Gentiles in Cornelius' house, he sat down and ate with them. This was in direct conflict to what he had previously preached.

It is interesting to notice how easy it is for people to succumb to societal pressures when it comes to matters of race. Often, people who have made conscious decisions to reach out to persons of a different background find themselves retreating to their old ways when others who have not been enlightened question their actions. The Apostle Paul rebuked Peter for this very reason.

After eating with Gentiles, Peter was called in question about this by the Jewish Christians at Jerusalem. They accused him of eating with "uncircumcised people" (Acts 10:28; 11:3). When prejudiced people came to Antioch, Peter refused to eat with the Gentiles for fear of offending Jews who had prejudice against the Gentiles. For giving in to the bigotry of others, Paul said that Peter, "was to be blamed." (Gal. 2:11-15)

It is never right to give in to bigotry, even for the so-called "sake of peace."

CHRISTIANS SHOULD NEVER SUCCUMB TO SOCIETAL PRESSURE

The cross of Jesus Christ should put away the attitude of bigotry. Through Christ, God has broken down the middle wall of partition between the Jew and all other nations of men. The Bible states that He "has put no difference between us whether we be Jew or Gentile." (Ephesians. 2:11,17; and 15:8,9)

There is no need to prove that there were Jew-Samaritan prejudices in Jesus' day. It is common knowledge that the Samaritans, who were considered "half-breeds", were a despised race. Of Jesus they charged, "Have we not said that you are a Samaritan and that you have a devil?" (John 8:48) This was an epithet that corresponds with calling a black man a "nigger" in our day. Jesus did not accept the Jewish feelings toward Samaritans. On one journey he purposely went through Samaria instead of traveling the traditional route, which would have avoided going through the land of this despised race. Jesus surprised a Samaritan woman with his request for a drink of water. She exclaimed, "Jews have no dealings with Samaritans!" How is it then that he talked with her? He could talk to her because he was not observing the prejudices of the mainstream crowd. He showed that a man's neighbor was anyone, Samaritan or not. Jews in Jesus' day crossed the Jordan to journey between Galilee and Judea. They would not pass through the hated and despised Samaritan territory. Jesus did not follow this prejudice but took his journey between Judea and Galilee through the heart of Samaria (John 4:4). Christ refused to succumb to the pressure from Jewish society to have no dealings with the Samaritans. Likewise, today's Christian must make a point of reaching out to those of other ethnic backgrounds, who may have historically been mistreated by members of their own race.

GOD'S REGARD FOR MAN IS BASED ON OBEDIENCE, NOT SKIN COLOR

In Genesis 4:4 God had respect to Abel and to his offering. Based on this some would claim that He had respect of persons. How does this harmonize with my proposition that God does not have respect of person? Note in Hebrews. 11:4 that Abel obtained a witness that he was righteous. Cain received the witness that he was evil. God had respect to Abel based on the way he lived his life. Likewise, God couldn't respect the way his brother Cain chose to represent himself. Therefore, God's respect was not based on the person, it was based on how the person represented himself before his Creator. God respects the actions of those who live right and does not respect the actions of those who do evil. (Romans. 2-3)

Jeremiah 38 and 39 record an incident where Jeremiah's life was threatened after cast into a well. Jeremiah's salvation came through the efforts of an African eunuch named Ebed Melech. Jeremiah was trapped in the muck in the well for several days before this Black man helped him out. Of everyone in Jerusalem who were supposed to be the chosen people of God at that time, only Jeremiah and a Black man who put his trust in God were saved from the wrath of King Nebuchadnezzar. No Jew was saved on that day. However, an Ethiopian, received the assurance that God has respect for him because he put his trust in God.

Paul's writing to the church at Ephesus (Ephesians 2:14-15) said that God broke down the middle wall of separation and abolished enmity. Racial barriers should never exist between people who share in Christian fellowship. There is no place in Christendom for preferences based on race, class, or culture. This is not acceptable to God. Sadly, those who choose to perpetuate the myth of inferiority continue to be selective about what the Bible says in order to establish a theological basis that justifies mistreatment of other people.

CHAPTER 4
THE MYTH OF
BLACK INFERIORITY

From its very beginning, a "supremacy" ideology has guided the actions of America. These views evolved out of deeply held convictions based on the misinterpretation of Scripture. American fathers worked from a theological base that established a doctrine that regarded whites as "God's elect." They were considered the embodiment of "God's chosen people." This interpretation of Scripture set them culturally above other nations and peoples. This combined with a commitment to fulfill their misguided mission of creating God's chosen society. This mission created the need for an economic base, which led to the first slaves being introduced soon after 1619. Slaves were justified, through their faulty interpretation of Scripture as part of a "heritage" for God's elect.[7]

The entire slavery movement was based on a belief in Black inferiority. Thomas Jefferson said, "I advance it therefore as a suspicion only, that the blacks, whether originally a distinct race, or made distinct by time and circumstance, are inferior to the whites in the endowments of body and mind." He stated on another occasion he felt the Negro "lacked native ability for the larger pursuits of civilization..."[8] Another proponent of slavery said, "Black people are incapable of self-government..." whereas, whites' skill at "organization and government are the sovereign tendencies of our race."[9] From its beginning, America has held a firm conviction that Black people were biologically and spiritually different and inferior to whites.

American scientists, politicians and theologians conspired to build an "apologetic" for the inferiority myth. The primary defense was based on science and theology.[10] Natural scientists such as Samuel George Norton studied physiological fields like "craniology" postulating that Blacks were inferior based on their brain being "smaller and lighter" than a Caucasians'. People accepted his so-called "scientific" foundation for the inferiority of Blacks and "superiority" of the White man because it didn't come from an emotional argument but emerged out of a conviction that this was part of nature's well ordered plan.

The notion of inherent Black inferiority has been reinforced in America through education. As "credible" scholars have rendered findings, they have been incorporated into professional journals of science and philosophy. History, as it has been taught in white society, has been altered to reinforce the natural superiority of the Caucasian race and of western European culture. In this sense, education has served the purpose of the western European institution. What was taught in academic settings was also taught at home and has become woven into the fabric of American society.[11]

The attitude of Christian people and leaders during the years of slavery and oppression is comparable to the years of Hitler's Germany. Through gradual acclimation, clergy and lay-people accepted the myth of Black inferiority little by little. When pressed to act against or on behalf of the issue, they responded as one church denomination had: "Slave holding is a civil institution; and we will not interfere. The character of civil institutions is governed by politics; and we will not interfere. Politics are beyond the scope of the church; and we will not interfere."[12]

Passive racism was fostered by inaction and by a society based on personal individualism instead of community and corporate responsibility. Because racism and slavery were viewed as institutional wrongs, individuals felt insulated from responsibility.[13] The same mentality escorted white Christian leaders through the civil rights years of the 1960's and still threatens us today.

"WHITENIZING" THE BIBLE TO SUPPORT BLACK INFERIORITY

In order to perpetuate the myth of inferiority, whites had to change the way people in the Bible were viewed. The manifest destiny of white people didn't allow them to acceptance the significance of roles played by other races, so "God and Jesus were overwhelmingly portrayed with European features."[14] A "whitenized" Church included defining Christianity in terms and images that are clearly western European.

Even today we are affected. "...When church history of other nations and especially third-world nations is taught, distortions and misinformation abound, for the premise is generally based on a mission theology that once considered these countries backward, pagan and uncivilized."[15]

To this day, slavery and the myth of Black inferiority affect American society. In his book, *Dismantling Racism*, Joseph Barnt defines racism as "prejudice with power."[16] He says racism is only present when a culture possesses the power to enforce its prejudices. Prejudice is defined as "Having opinions without knowing the facts or to hold on to these opinions, even after contrary facts are known." Based on this definition racism is a problem of the dominant social institution. To be blunt, he states "racism is a white problem, not a black problem." He elaborates, "If there had been no racism in America, there would be no racial churches. As it is, we have white churches and black churches; white denominations and black denominations; American Christianity and black religion." It all exacerbates our relationships and builds-in perpetuation of the problem.

THE COST OF AMERICAN RACISM

White America has sown seeds of destruction throughout the world, yet as a nation America has the audacity to be appalled by the abuses of other regimes, the Holocaust, the Killing Fields of Southeast Asia, and the reign of Iraqi leader Saddam Hussein. What about America? What has been the accumulated cost in lives attributable to the myth of white superiority and Black inferiority? One estimate suggests that in the 350 years since America's first colonies were established, over six million "people of color" which includes Native-Americans and African-Americans, have been *killed* to carry out the "God given" destiny of America.[17] America should recall the words of Thomas Jefferson, "*Indeed I tremble for my country when I reflect that God is just: that his justice cannot sleep forever...*"[18]

THE BLACK PRESENCE IN THE BIBLE

While much focus has been placed on the relationship of Black people to the sons of Ham, the record of history and the Bible reveals a heritage that we seldom hear about related to black peoples in the Bible.

MOSES

You might recall the story of Joseph, son of Jacob who ended up governing much of Egypt. He married a black "Ethiopian" woman and their children were included in Israeli tribal inheritance. When the Israelites finally left Egypt, 500,000 of their people accompanied. That population developed from intermarriage with Egyptians, permission to do so, given from God.

Moses grew up in the court of the dark-skinned pharaoh of Egypt following the enslavement of the Israelites. At the period of Moses' life, he was married also to a woman of black descent and had sons of mixed ancestry as well. Jethro his father-in-law, a black man, was responsible for instituting the organization of government for Israel. (Genesis 39-50; Exodus 2-3; 18:1-12; Numbers 12:1)

No More Cursing

DAVID AND SOLOMON

David's great-grandmother was Rahab a Black Canaanite. His grandmother was a dark-skinned Moabite named Ruth. His son Solomon was born from his wife Bathsheba, who is linked to her tribal roots of "Sheba" a Hamitic people.

JESUS

The most exciting link for anyone with an African heritage should be to know that Jesus had at least four generations, of dark-skinned or "Black" ancestry in his heritage. His genealogy found in Matthew 1:1-16 lists only five women. Four of them: Tamar, Rahab, Ruth and Bathsheba were from Hamitic groups and were Black. Some scholars note that all Biblical ethnic heritages can be traced through Jesus lineage.[19]

CHRISTIAN HISTORY

Following Jesus death and resurrection, the first Christian convert outside of Judaism was a high official in the Ethiopian government (Acts 8:27-38). The Coptic Church, which is the oldest Christian church outside of Palestine, draws its history from that encounter. Following the death of the Apostles, 6 of the 12 early church fathers, including Augustine, were from Alexandria and north African cities, which was the center of doctrine *before Rome*. Church historian Kenneth Scott Latourette says, "On the north shore of Africa west of Egypt, and especially in and around Carthage in the present Tunis and Algeria, Christianity was very strong..."[20] The foundation of modern Christianity was established on the African continent.

CHAPTER 5
LESSONS FROM SAMARIA

It would seem that in the twenty-first century, America would have properly addressed the problems of race and racism. Yet, in spite of its boast of being a melting pot, this problem continues to plague American society.

Today, prominent White Christian leaders continue to say that, based on the "curse of Ham," black people are under God's judgment. Across the country, racial tensions in our communities continue to rise while racial divisions within their churches prevent the Christian community from properly addressing these problems. Dr. Martin Luther King Jr. was right: "either we must learn to live together as brothers or we will certainly die together as fools."

Why has there been so little progress in race relations in American culture in general and American Christianity in particular? Four things continue to block our progress: (1) cultural prejudice; (2) the fear of losing racial distinctions; (3) the hesitancy to hold people accountable for racial prejudice; and (4) the fear of the price tag of unity;

CULTURAL PREJUDICE

A major hindrance to Christian unity is the authority given to cultural diversity. Often Black Christians are guilty of amalgamating the tenets of their culture with their faith. Often, we blame White racism for what really is our own irresponsibility. Black people cannot continue to appeal to white oppression to excuse their ineptness. Blacks are not such a weak, powerless, and ungifted people that they can only function to the degree white people allow them. Conversely, some whites ignore their Bible when it comes to protecting their traditions. Isn't it amazing how some white Christians embrace Black people until they find out that their child is interested in dating or marrying one? All of a sudden, questions like, "what about the children?" and "what will the relatives think?" arise instead of questions concerned with what the Bible says. In both of these perspectives people have failed to recognize biblical authority when it clashes with cultural or racial presuppositions.

THE FEAR OF LOSING OUR RACIAL DISTINCTION

We must realize that unity does not equal sameness. Just as a husband and wife can become one, cultures and races can be one without being the same. In order to have unity, or to achieve the essence of oneness, both parties must be willing to move in one direction for the common good of everyone. When differing cultures establish private agendas that don't involve the overall good of everyone, society is in trouble. As Christians we must have a unified purpose.

THE HESITANCY TO HOLD PEOPLE ACCOUNTABLE FOR RACIAL PREJUDICE

Every Christian must hold other Christians accountable for refusing to cooperate with bridge-building efforts. The church cannot condone racial slurs and public rejection of people based on their differences. There is no time for Christians to sit by passively and wait for people to change. People must be led into change, and that cannot be done without knowing that they will be held accountable for how they treat other members of God's family. Only when the body of Christ is willing to take this stand will the effort toward racial reconciliation and harmony be worthwhile. For one side to pay the price without equal commitment from the other will only create more mistrust and division. When both sides take a strong biblical stand the support systems will be there to withstand the opposition that will naturally come.

THE FEAR OF THE PRICE TAG OF UNITY

The cost of unity is another problem that must be addressed. Unity is expensive. People of different races must be willing to pay the price for Christian unity. We must be willing to experience the rejection of friends and relatives, whether Christians or non-Christians, who are not willing to accept that spiritual family relationships transcend physical, cultural, and racial relationships. This is what Jesus meant when he said, "whoever does the will of my Father in heaven is my brother and sister and mother" (Matthew. 12:50). The cost is particularly expensive to local churches who begin opening their doors to people who are viewed by many as socially unacceptable, even though they have been made acceptable to the Father by the blood of Christ.

In order to prepare for God's unity call, pastors must begin preaching the whole counsel of God on the issue of racism (James 2:1-13). We are going to have to remind our congregations of Ephesians 2:14, "For he himself is our peace, who has made the two one and has destroyed the barrier, the dividing of hostility...." We are going to have to stop ignoring the parable of the Good Samaritan, Christ's teaching on the responsibility of people to demonstrate love tangibly for a neighbor, even if the neighbor is from a different culture (Luke 10:30-37). The Christian church must follow up with practical opportunities for bridging the cultural divide.

WHAT DOES SAMARIA TEACH US?

One of the most poignant and informative teachings regarding culture, truth, and unity is the story of Jesus' encounter with the woman of Samaria in John 4. This story gives us two overriding principles needed to reach true biblical unity: (1) we must establish common ground, and (2) we must refuse to allow our cultures to interfere with God's truth.

When Jesus traveled with his disciples through Samaria, he was not merely taking a shorter route. He was on a mission to meet needs he knew existed there. The fact that he entered Samaria made it clear he was willing to go beyond his own culture to meet those needs. Overcoming the cultural prejudice of the Samaritans was another issue. Jesus was willing to make the first move. In order to get the Samaritans to give him the opportunity to minister to them he had to establish common ground, which is the first principle for Christian unity.

In Samaria, Jesus rested at Jacob's well (John 4:6). It was a natural place for someone who was hot and tired to stop. However, Jesus chose this particular well because both the Jews and the Samaritans loved Jacob, who was the father of both groups. He stopped at Jacob's well and built a bridge of communication by starting with what he and the Samaritan woman could agree on.

As he spoke to the woman at the well, Jesus did not enter into an analysis of the cultural differences between Jews and Samaritans, but rather He moved to the spiritual issue of the woman's need for forgiveness. He allowed her to hold on to her history, culture, and experience as a Samaritan. Yet he established common ground. Similarly, Christians of all races and cultures today need to establish common ground. Our common ground is based on our love of Jesus Christ.

The second principle for Christian unity is that Jesus refused to allow culture to interfere with his higher priority of representing God's truth. When the Samaritan woman allowed her cultural background to cloud her correct understanding about God, Jesus immediately rejected her cultural commitment. In rather direct language, Jesus said to the woman, "You Samaritans worship what you do not know" (John

4:22). His point was acutely clear: Whenever there is a conflict between culture and God's truth, culture must always submit to the truth of God as revealed in his Word. When the woman's culture crossed sacred lines, Christ invaded her world to condemn it and let her know that her father, grandfather, and great-grandfather were all wrong.

This means that to refer to oneself as a Black Christian, White Christian, Mexican Christian, or Chinese Christian is technically incorrect. Our Christianity should never be modified by our culture. Our Christianity should modify our culture. We must see ourselves as Christian Blacks, Christian Whites, Christian Mexicans, or Christian Chinese.

Whenever we make the adjective Black, White, Brown, and Yellow descriptive of Christians, it may mean we have changed Christianity to make it fit a cultural description. The Bible teaches the opposite—that we are Christians who may happen to be Black, White, Brown, or Yellow. If anything changes, it is to be our cultural orientation, not our Christianity.

Jesus not only critiqued the Samaritan culture by the truth of God's Word, but he critiqued his own Jewish culture by that same standard. When his disciples complained that he was talking with a Samaritan woman, he rejected their racism by telling them it was more important for him to do the will of God than to succumb to their biases (John 4:31-34). Obeying the will of God always takes a priority over satisfying cultural expectations.

In the Black community, there are cultural trademarks. For example, we have special ways of saluting one another, shaking hands, and communicating in general. Although these marks of cultural identification and racial solidarity are acceptable, they cannot supersede spiritual identification. Therefore, Christians of different races and cultures must learn that spiritual relationship forms the basis for true brotherhood. This is so because the bond between Christians of different races is eternal, whereas the relationship between a Christian and non-Christian of the same race is temporal.

THE CHRISTIAN AGENDA

Jesus makes a powerful statement in John 13:35 when he says, "All men will know that you are my disciples if you love one another." This implies two critical principles: First, Christians are to make something happen in their relationship with each other that is so dynamic that the world will view it as worth looking into. And second, our love for one another should be public, so unbelievers can see that Christianity is not a secret.

God does not require that all churches are integrated, but he does require that all function harmoniously as the body of Christ without divisiveness. Jesus is not asking Blacks to become whites or whites to become Asians or Latinos to become Native Americans, but he insists that all reflect God's truth as given in Scripture. When culture does not infringe upon the Word of God, we are free to be what God has created us to be, with all the uniqueness that accompanies our cultural heritage.

However, the objective truth from Scripture places limits on our cultural experience. As African-Americans continue to seek cultural freedom, we must examine every strategy offered to promote justice under the magnifying glass of Scripture. Every bit of advice given by our leaders and all definitions proposing to tell us what it means to be Black must be commensurate with divine revelation.

Whites, too, must submit their cultural traditions to the authority of God's Word if they are going to play their part in dismantling their contribution to the racial mythology that is a dominant theme in their worldview.

The bottom line is that there must be a moral frame of reference through which both Black and white experiences are examined and judged, and the only standard that qualifies is the Bible.

CHAPTER 6

THE CURSE OF HAM

The source of much of the prejudice against African Americans within the Christian Church and in American society is due to the erroneous "curse of Ham" myth. This myth has been used to justify the arguments associated with bigotry and is the most widespread justification for the current and past discrimination and dehumanization of Black people. Most Bible students have been exposed to the despicable notion that the Scriptures uphold a subservient position for Black people. For far too long, the curse of servitude recorded in Genesis 9 has been wrongly applied to African Americans to rid Americans of the guilt of slavery and oppression.

Today, many so-called Christians still hold to the notion that the descendants of Africans are destined to be servants and should accept their second-class status as the fulfillment of biblical prophecy. Clergy and laity alike have touted this as the biblical reason why Black must endure the humiliation of American racism and look for relief in the "great bye and bye."

Bibles, such as the Scofield Reference Bible endorsed the curse of Ham theory, causing widespread acceptance on the basis that "trained theologians" supported it.

This false biblical interpretation, coupled with the history of slavery, oppression, segregation, and discrimination in America, has firmly embedded the inferiority of Black people in the psyche of people of all walks of life, sadly, Black people included.

MYTHS DON'T HAVE TO BE SUPPORTED BY FACTS

It is interesting to note the portions of scripture that have been ignored in order to advance the curse of Ham. The supporters of the curse have ignored the fact that the Bible says that Canaan, Ham's son, was cursed. They ignore the fact that in Exodus 20:5 the Bible places a time limitation of three to four generations on curses. They ignore the biblical plight of the Canaanites, who were defeated by Israel, as the potential fulfillment of the curse. They also ignore the fact that the descendants of Ham's three other sons continue to live today in Ethiopia (Cush), Egypt (Mizraim), and Lybia (Phut).

It is obvious that myths such as the curse of Ham don't need to be based on facts, they simple need people willing to support them. The supporters of the curse of Ham have used other parts of the Bible to corroborate their claim of Black inferiority. New Testament texts such as Ephesians 6:5-8 and Colossians 3:22 were used to prove "God's desire" for Black slaves to obey their white masters. These supporters included clergy and religious heroes. They taught Black slaves to accept their fate as the will of God. Anything else would be considered rebellion against God and result in eternal damnation.

As religious leaders taught the myth of inferiority, it became "sound" theological doctrine. Scriptural texts such as Philemon 1:15-16 and 1 Corinthians 7:21, which taught masters to treat converted slaves as equal brothers and that slaves could change their status, were totally ignored. As far as these curse supporters were concerned, it was a slave master's right to treat a slave anyway he deemed appropriate.

AMERICA AND THE CURSE OF HAM

The United States of America has come to symbolize the principles of democracy, capitalism and free trade while portraying itself as a place of freedom, justice, and equality. However, for many of its citizens, America represents far less than those ideals. One of the great dichotomies regarding this country is how it can be the wealthiest, most powerful, most Christian, and most democratic nation while being perhaps the most oppressive and most racist nation at the same time.

While the mainstream portrays America the beautiful, voices from outside the mainstream speak of America the ugly. The mainstream speaks of great wealth while another voice scream of poverty. The mainstream boasts of America's fight for peace across the globe while others within its own borders complain about violence. Many brag about America's colleges and universities while others tell their story of being locked out of the educational systems and being forced to live in ignorance and self-hatred. Worst of all, the mainstream sticks its chest out while talking about America as a place that was founded on freedom of religion while others testify that America's religion has been the harbinger of racial hatred and other atrocities too many to name. The mainstream talks about a melting pot where all are welcome and treated equally while those in the margins regard America as a frying pan, hot with the grease of white supremacy.

White supremacy is the oil that lubricates the engine of American culture. It has become so ingrained in American society that at times it goes unnoticed. It has become the ideology of American capitalism and religion. Sadly, religious racism is rooted in white supremacy. Genesis 9:18-27 has served as the biblical foundation upon which supremacy, slavery, racism, and oppression has been built.

The mythological curse of Ham has been the link between American slavery and oppression and people with Black skin. While Americans didn't invent the myth, its ideals were escalated within the context of American slavery. The 1852 Studies on Slavery in Easy Lessons, written by John Fletchers from Mississippi, stated, "It was only right therefore that the degenerate black descendants of Ham were doomed to perpetual servitude to the superior white offspring of Shem and Japheth."

No More Cursing

THE SILENCE OF MAINSTREAM WHITE CHRISTIAN CHURCHES

Religious racism in America has assigned second-class status to Black people and perpetuated white supremacy. It has become so imbedded in the American psyche that even those who ideologically oppose racial discrimination do little to oppose it. Few white Christians have been willing to leave their comfort zones and critique the theology of white supremacy upon which their churches and Western Christianity has been established.

The silence of American Christians to racist teachings and actions has given consent to systems that oppress and exploit Black people. The ideology of racism has become so internalized that few people within Christendom are aware of the obvious contradictions between their everyday and religious practices and the Bible to which they give allegiance. Their oblivion to the inherent racism within their religious tradition makes it nearly impossible to change it.

THE BLACK CHURCH HAS REINTERPRETED THE CURSE OF HAM

The Black church has sought to transform the theology of white supremacy by offering an alternative interpretation of what the Bible says. While white racist continue their historic use of the Bible as a weapon of oppression, Black theologians use it to fight against the very oppression that their counterparts declare is "the will of God." Blacks have rejected the formally accepted notion that they were

An Artist's Depiction of Noah Cursing Ham

destined by God to be inferior and interpreted the Bible against the backdrop of their struggles.

Blacks have seen the 1863 Emancipation Proclamation as the hand of God intervening on their behalf. How else could Blacks have been freed? It had to be the Lord to pit white men against each other for the freedom of Black people. This historical instance, along with the Biblical Exodus of Israel from Egypt helped to support an ideology that God is on the side of the oppressed.

Black theologians have rarely denied that the "curse of Ham" existed, they have simply attempted to reinterpret the way it has been taught. A close look at the Biblical text exposes the fact that racism and bigotry have been the catalysts for taking the Scripture out of context:

"And Ham, the father of Canaan, saw the nakedness

of his father and told his two brothers without. And Shem and Japheth took a garment and laid it on both their shoulders and covered the nakedness of their father. And Noah awoke from his wine and knew what his youngest son had done unto him. And he said, "Cursed be Canaan, a servant of servants shall he be to his brethren. And he said, Blessed be the LORD God of Shem and Canaan shall be his servant. God shall enlarge Japheth and he shall dwell in the tents of Shem and Canaan shall be his servant." (Genesis 9:24-27)

This story describes how Noah, after getting off the ark, made wine and got drunk. In his drunken state, Noah exposed himself. His son Ham saw him naked and told his brothers Shem and Japeth. Ham's brothers went and covered Noah's nakedness. When Noah found out what Ham did, he cursed his son Canaan with slavery and blessed Ham's brothers.

The tenth chapter of Genesis, known as the table of nations, has been studied by archaeologists as well as Bible students. It records the names of the nations who came from each of the sons of Noah, --Shem, Ham, and Japheth.

WHO WAS CURSED?

In Genesis 9, only two sons of Noah, Shem and Japheth are mentioned in the curse. Ham was never mentioned in any way, shape or form. The text reveals that Canaan, Ham's son, was mentioned as the recipient of the curse. Ham's three other sons were not mentioned, therefore were not recipients of the curse. The Scripture specifically states "Cursed be Canaan, a servant of servants shall he be."

NOAH'S PROPHECY

The prophecy states: "Blessed be the LORD God of Shem." The fulfillment of this is realized through God making choice of Shem's descendants as the line through which Jesus Christ would be born. Thus, the Hebrew people are called Semitic.

For approximately 2200 years, a period that extended from the call of Abraham until the death of Jesus Christ, God was "the Lord God of Shem."

Next, the prophecy states: "God shall enlarge Japheth and he shall dwell in the tents of Shem." The descendants of Japeth are generally considered Caucasian people. Since Biblical times, Japhetic people have dominated civilization through war and the conquering of other nations. History will bear witness that white people have dominated people of other races.

For nearly 2200 years God was exclusively the God of Shem, and the descendants of Shem were the vessels through which God spoke to the world. Shortly after the death and resurrection of Christ, Christianity became a religion dominated by Japethic people. Embraced by the Roman Emperor Constantine, Christianity became the official religion of Rome and began to spread across the world. The prophecy truly records that Japheth does "dwell in the tents of Shem", as Japhetic people have, in many instances, become witnesses for Christ in the place of Semitic people.

No More Cursing

HAMITIC PEOPLE

The descendants of Ham, or Hamitic people, are listed in Genesis 10:6. They include Cush, Mizraim, Phut, and Canaan. The word "Ham" means hot, dark, or swarthy. From the sons of Ham came the Ethiopians, descendants of Cush, the Egyptians, descendants of Mizraim, and the Canaanites. All of these people would be considered Black people.

The word "Cush" in Hebrew is used synonymously with "Ethiopia" in the most English translations of the Bible. Jeremiah asked, "Can the Ethiopian change his skin?" (Jeremiah. 13:23) The Cushite people originally settled in the Mesopotamian Valley where they developed the world's first civilization. Later, descendants of Shem became the race of power in Mesopotamia after invasions. Mesopotamian Cushites are known as Sumerians in secular history.

Nimrod, a descendant of Cush, was the builder of some of the greatest cities of the ancient world. He was the founder of Nineveh, Babylon, Erech, and Acid. Any true student of history is familiar with these civilizations. The fact that a Black man founded them flies in the face of conventional wisdom that Black people were uncivilized until taken captive and made to be slaves in America. Biblical and secular history bears witness to the fact that great cultures were developed by Black people, the descendants of Ham.

Hamitic people were conquered and driven out of Mesopotamia by Semitic people around 1900 B.C. This may have been the catalyst to their migration to other parts of Africa and elsewhere. The Cushites, though sons and daughters of Ham, were not recipients of the curse recorded in Genesis Chapter 9. The second son of Ham, Mizraim, is the Hebrew name for Egypt. Egypt is the second Old World civilization that followed Mesopotamia. The pyramids and glories of the dynasties of ancient Egypt are legendary. Contrary to Hollywood depictions, these wonders were the product of dark-skinned Hamitic people. Statues, paintings, and other artifacts clearly depict the pharaohs and other Egyptians as people with Hamitic features. King Tutankhamen and Amenhotep are examples of men possessing Hamitic features.

It often amazes me when Caucasians writers and film producers attempt to rewrite history by depicting the people of ancient Egyptian civilization as white people while only depicting Black people as slaves or savages. The history and ability of African people is called in question in order to promote the superiority of Caucasian people. So-called white historians have erroneously credited the Caucasian race with developing the civilizations of Egypt, Assyria, Sumeria, Chaldea, Babylon, Persia, India, Palestine, Phoenicia, and Carthage. None of these civilizations trace their origins to Japhetic (Caucasian) people.

Psalm 105:27 records: "God did great wonders in the land of Ham." This was an obvious reference to the ten plagues of Egypt. Egyptians were known as Hamites. They are not Canaanites, the people whom Noah cursed in Genesis 9.

Phut, the third son of Ham is commonly thought to have been the progenitor of peoples around Libya by historians and Bible students. As with Cush and

Mizraim, Phut was not a part of the curse.

Canaan, Ham's fourth son, was the person cursed by Noah. Canaan's descendants are listed in the tenth chapter of Genesis. They are listed as Sidon, Hittites, Jebusites, Amorites, Girgashites, Hivites, Sinites, etc. Genesis 10:19 records the border of the Canaanites as being "from Sidon as you come to Gerar unto Gaza, as you go unto Sodom and Gomorrah and Admah and Zeboim and Laisha." If you were to trace this on a map it would reveal the area now known as the Holy Land. It is also know as the Promised Land, the area that God promised to Abraham. The ancient people who lived in that land were the people whom Noah cursed when he said, "Cursed be Canaan, a servant of servants shall he be to his brothers."

The fact that the Cushites and the descendants of Mizraim and Phut, all Black people, were not parts of the Noahic curse contradicts the absurd notion that Black skin is related to the Biblical curse. Likewise, the slavery and oppression of African American people in the United States or in any other part of the world has no foundation in the Sacred Scriptures.

THE CURSE

While we have clearly seen the fulfillment of Noah's prophecy concerning the descendants of both Shem and Japeth, we have been less clear whether or not the curse on the descendants of Canaan has been manifested. Thus, it has become easy for bigots and those who do not accurately interpret the Bible to pass off the oppression of Black people as the fulfillment of Biblical prophecy.

The Canaanites and their descendants are mentioned in Genesis 12:12-16 as the inhabitants of the land that God promised to Abraham. God then renewed this promise from time to time to assure Abraham of the certainty of the fulfillment of His word. Abraham lived his whole life believing God's promise, though during his lifetime he would never see the possession of the land.

In Genesis 15 the Bible details the reason the promise was deferred:

"Know of a surety that your seed shall be a stranger in a land that is not theirs, and shall serve them and they shall afflict them four hundred years...But in the fourth generation they shall come hither again, For the iniquity of the Amorites is not yet full... Unto your seed have I given the land from the river of Egypt unto the great river, the river Euphrates...the Hittites, Perizzites, Amorites, Canaanites, Girgashites, Jebusites."(Genesis 15:13, 16, 18, 20, 21).

THE INIQUITY OF THE AMORITES IS NOT FULL

In other words, they are not evil enough to bring upon them the curse that was first spoken by Noah. But by the fourth generation they would be. These are the people who, if any, were cursed. God disregarded the ownership of the land of Canaan (the cursed people) and gave it to Abraham (the father of the blessed people). This promise to give the land, and mentioning the names of the same Canaanite tribes is again recorded in Exodus 3:8 where Moses is informed and again in Exodus 13:5, "The LORD will bring you into the land of the Canaanites." And in Exodus 23:23,24 "For mine angel shall go before you unto the Amorites and the Hittites, Canaanites...and I will cut them off...you shall utterly overthrow them." Who? The cursed people.

The twelve spies that Joshua sent out before invading Palestine brought report of the Canaanites (the cursed people) dwelling in the Promised Land in strong cities by the Jordan. (Numbers 21:1-3) There God helped the Israelites exterminate the Canaanites in that area. This development is detailed in Deuteronomy 7:1.

"When the Lord your God shall bring you into the land where you are to possess it and has cast out many nations before you: the Hittites, the Girgashites, the Amorites, the Canaanites, the Perizzites, and the Hivites, and the Jebusites: seven nations greater and mightier than you. And when the LORD shall deliver them before you, you shall smite them and utterly destroy them."

The conclusions are clear: Canaanites, not all Hamitic people, were cursed. The Canaanites received that which fulfilled the prophetic curse when the Hebrews invaded the land of Canaan. Therefore Black people, in spite of the abuses of "Christian" white men, have not inherited the Curse of Canaan.

POTENCY OF THE "CURSE" HAS NOT BEEN UNDERMINED

Despite this fact, and evidence to prove it, the potency of the curse in the minds of people has not been undermined. The demise of slavery and legal segregation has not eradicated the effects of its teaching. Like a disease, the curse has mutated and survives in the hearts and minds of people everywhere. Contrary to those who think America has effectively dealt with its race problem, teachings like the curse simply lay dormant rather than dead. Occasionally we hear people refer to it on the television and radio waves. We hear it in religious discourse and see it in the writings of so-called theologians. It was only after negative publicity sparked by the Rev. Dr. Frederick K.C. Price's teaching series on race in 1998 did Dake Publishing announce its intent to remove remarks that could be considered racist and its affirmation of the curse from the *Dake Annotated Reference Bible*. Sadly, they have only gone through the motions as their revised version contains the same information under a different subtitle.

It would be naïve for us to regard the curse as a thing of the past or to believe that people have stopped using the Bible to justify war and oppression. Teachings such as this are a like a cancer, they must be discharged from the body in a radical way. America's problems with race relations are in need of spiritual healing. Sadly, America's spiritual leaders have been the leading proponents of teachings that foster racism and discrimination.

DEFLECTING THE CURSE FROM HAM TO CANAAN DOES LITTLE TO SOLVE THE PROBLEM

Despite two hundred years of attacks and efforts by preachers, teachers, authors, and Biblical scholars, the myth of the curse still survives in American culture. One reason for its persistence is that many of these attacks have only focused on the curse's application to Black people instead of the flawed teaching on the curse itself. The gist of most attacks on the curse is to claim that American blacks are not the descendants of Canaan, as I have argued earlier in this chapter. This strategy rightfully argues that American Blacks are descendants of Cush and Mizraim and were not part of Noah's curse. The problem with stopping at this point leaves the impression that the curse remains in effect on the descendants of Canaan. What we unfortunately imply is that three-fourths of the descendants of Ham are exempt from the curse and the remaining one-fourth is not exempt. Therefore, this strategy has done little to stop racist readings of Genesis 9-11.

THE SAME TEXT AFFIRMS
THE EQUALITY OF BLACKS

We must utilize the same text that has been used to justify racism to disarm it. Isn't it ironic that Genesis 9-11, while misinterpreted by those who wish to promote Black inferiority, is the same text that affirms Black humanity? This same text is the basis for regarding all humans as descendants from the same parents. Therefore, if everyone can trace their lineage back to Noah, how can any race be superior when they all have the same genetic make-up? Despite its use to justify slavery and oppression and to vilify Black people, this text establishes the humanity of all of Ham's descendants.

DID NOAH ACT ON GOD'S BEHALF?

Although I have touched on this subject somewhat, I want to spend a little more time on the fact that the curse recorded in Genesis 9 did not originate with God.

If we placed the ninth chapter of Genesis in context with the proceeding eight chapters we would expect that God's voice would be heard if he were to pass judgment on Ham or Canaan. In every instance where judgment was passed before this instance, God made the declaration Himself. From the fall of Adam to the sin of Cain to the wickedness of the people in Noah's time, God expressed his disapproval and judgment. In light of this, we must ask why God was quiet for the first time in biblical history. Instead of God, Noah speaks the curse. Those words are the only words spoken by Noah in the entire Biblical record. Ironically, they are words that have had quite an impact throughout history.

Most interpretations imply that God spoke through Noah in this instance. This is based on Noah's authority and the Scriptural description of him as "a righteous man, blameless in his generation" (Gen. 6:9). Therefore, most readers have concluded that Noah's curse is indeed God's curse. Despite the description of Noah as a "blameless" man, the fact remains that he was in a drunken state and that the text gives no indication that he was acting as an agent for God.

It seems to make little difference whether the curse is an act of man or God. As I stated before, myths don't have to be supported by facts, just believed.

No More Cursing

Whenever a curse finds believers, it becomes realized. However, we must determine the difference between God's will and Noah's will. The nature of God is one that allows redemption. What kind of God would allow every generation of a people to be cursed based upon the actions of one man?

Those who interpret his actions as synonymous with God's have considered Noah untouchable. The irony of this interpretation is that it ignores his humanness, which is evident by the fact that he was drunk and naked in the first place. While some scholars assert that Ham sexually assaulted his father, the text doesn't affirm that position.

THE CURSE AS A SCAPEGOAT

The curse has been used to blame Black people for their oppression and mistreatment. After all, If it weren't for the behavior of your ancestor Ham, you wouldn't be treated the way your are, right? America's white supremist society has an uncanny knack for "blaming the victim." Through the collective act of scapegoating, disorder has been transferred from the guilty community to the victim. This discrepancy, which has troubled generations of readers, is actually evidence that many have taken pains to transform Ham from an arbitrary victim to a dangerous criminal. Racists have used Genesis 9 as a scapegoat for their heinous crimes toward Black people.

As victims of America's racist attitudes, Black people have been used as scapegoats. They have functioned as sacrificial victims by being killed, marginalized and abandoned. The historical use of the curse has made

Black people into perpetual human sacrifices, targets of whatever racist need to account for.

The historical interpretation of Genesis 9-11 by the Christian church has been one that vilifies the entire Black race. Black people have become victims of a culture fueled by racism and the biblical myths that sustain it.

GIVING HAM A VOICE

Opponents of the curse must do more than deflect it from Ham to Canaan. We must give Ham a voice. Ham, as opposed to tradition interpretation of the text, was a victim and not a victimizer. Listen as Ham tells his story:

"I am the true victim in this story because I committed no crime. Here is what happened: After we got off the ark we took some time away from each other to enjoy some personal time. When the waters ebbed we got into a daily routine. Dad took care of the grapevines. He often drank of their fruit after they fermented. Dad used to have nightmares about the flood. I heard him because my tent was closest to his. My two older brothers shared a tent on the other side of our fathers. They had a sibling rivalry going, each one trying to outdo the other for Dad's approval. I didn't know that their actions would eventually get me into trouble.

I think Dad would drink a lot to help him deal with the guilt he felt about his family being the only one to survive the flood. All of our friends and neighbors were killed and he had a hard time dealing with it. One night after we all went to bed I heard Dad moaning so I peeked into his tent. When I looked in I saw Dad lying on the floor completely naked. He was talking in his sleep and had obviously been drinking.

Eventually, Dad got so loud that he woke my brothers. When they came to see what was going on. I told them that Dad was having a dream and was lying on the floor naked. They both wanted to go in and cover Dad up in order to get credit for coming to his aid. They fought over a blanket before finally going in side by side to cover Dad up.

The next morning Dad called us in order to announce his paternal blessings. First he blessed Shem, the oldest—no surprise there; but then he blessed Japheth, too. He said that Japheth could dwell in Shem's tents. Next he said that my son Canaan was going to serve both of them. I couldn't believe what he said.

It was obvious that Dad was confused and upset about what happened the night before. He thought I had dishonored him by laughing about his nakedness and spreading word about it. I did tell my brothers about it, however, it was never meant to dishonor him. He also accused me of sexual indiscretion during the night. The fact that he got drunk gave some level of credibility to his story.

However, his story was full of holes. He couldn't make up his mind whether it was me or Canaan who tried to take away his manhood. My brothers believed the whole story and were delighted to get their blessing and then gang up on me. With Dad making up stories about me to hide the fact that he was in a drunken stupor, I left and never came back home. It is unfortunate that my family tells such crazy stories about me."

THE CURSE TODAY

It is obvious that Genesis 9:20-27 has no application in the contemporary world. However, this text speaks about more than Noah's nakedness and the history of the Israelites vilifying Canaanites. Ham's identity as a scapegoat and a victim represent a revelatory trace in the story. From a Christian perspective, Ham is a type of Christ. His family forced him into victimhood as Jesus chooses victimhood in order to expose the violent foundations of his culture. Ham's innocence is not immediately vindicated by God, but must be unveiled by the constant retelling of his story.

Chapter 7

CONFRONTING
RACISM IN RELIGION

In order to determine how race relates to the Christian worldview we must take a look at the issue of race in the framework of the Great Commission. The command of Christ to His disciples was to, "Go and make disciples of all the nations." The word "nations" is *ethnoi* in Greek, and means "ethnic groups." The Apostle John also uses the word "nations" when describing Heaven in Revelation 7:9. There he sees a great multitude which no one could number, of all nations, kindreds, peoples, and tongues, standing before the throne of God, clothed with white robes, with palm branches in their hands. While the word "race" is not mentioned, it is implied. This description teaches us that Church gathered around God's throne is a unified, integrated Church. Paul teaches in Ephesians 2 that Christ has "broken down the middle wall of separation." Therefore, we are all members of the one household of God and must come to an important truth about race: The Church on earth and the Church in heaven belong to one family made up of all races of the earth.

If this is true, why was a Civil rights movement necessary in America? It was necessary because the normal social interactions among people of different races were poisoned. In America, Blacks could not eat in the same restaurants, use the same restrooms or be treated in the same hospital wards as Whites. The races were legally separated in public transportation, in schools, in waiting rooms, hotels, theaters, cemeteries, parks, courtrooms, drinking fountains, and every other public area

The notion that the races should be separated resulted in reprehensible practices throughout the country. Florida made it illegal to give white pupils textbooks that had previously been used by black students. Oklahoma required separate telephone booths for the two races. Many states contended that the touch of a Black person would defile a white person.

Schools attended by Blacks were substandard. Whites believed that educating Blacks was dangerous. Legislators were said to be careful about the amount of money spent to educate Blacks because, in their minds, to educate Blacks was to "ruin good cotton pickers."

Because they were required to ride at the back of buses, Blacks had first to enter at the front and pay their fare, and then get off the bus and proceed to the back door to find a seat.

Black people were referred to by the racial slur "nigger." This term isolated Blacks from mainstream society as it established them as "less than human." Whites referred to grown Black men as "boy" and women as "girl." Older Blacks were called "uncle" or "auntie." When letters sent to black men or women were addressed with the title "Mr." or "Mrs.", the post office took the liberty to cross out those titles. A title of respect used to address Blacks was forbidden.

Racism in America has been a type of pathological madness that, in its vilest form, resulted in outright murder. Many Blacks were lynched at the hands of white mobs without benefit of trial, judge or jury. Every Black in the country was terrorized by the potential of being lynched.

WHERE DOES CHURCH FIT IN THE HISTORY OF RACISM?

Where does the church fit in this history of racism in America? As mentioned in the first chapter, the Black churches played a crucial role. The activism of Black ministers demonstrated that Christianity could be a catalyst for social change. Conversely, it is shameful that the majority of white churches chose not to get involved in the Civil Rights movement. There are several reasons for the white church abdicating its responsibility to fight the evil of racism; however, the most reprehensible reason lies in the church's justification for slavery, segregation, and subjugation on Biblical grounds. Major elements of racism espoused by the church that have become a part of the white American's belief system include the following:

- **Biological source of culture.** Culture and civilization are products of the biological endowments of each race.

- **Nonwhite = low status roles.** Since non-white races are considered naturally inferior it is appropriate that are limited to low status, which they should be satisfied with.

- **White race = high culture.** The development of a high culture is the natural product of a superior white race. This is the argument for white supremacy.

- **Racial purity is of utmost importance.** Racial purity must be preserved at all costs. The white race must maintain their current position of power.

- **Race mixing = decay.** Mixing of the races will lead to a deterioration of the dominant white culture.

- **Inequality of the races**. Races are unequal and have been made that way by God Himself.

RACISM SPREAD BY DAKE'S ANNOTATED REFERENCE BIBLE

Although these beliefs about of race find little or no support in theological, biological or scientific scholarship, they are racial myths that continue to justify the system of racism that has become commonplace in American society.

While there are many so-called Christian leaders who have helped perpetuate a racist belief system, I want to focus for a moment on the views of Finis Jennings Dake.

Dake (1902-1987) was a Pentecostal fundamentalist minister who rejected formal training and traditional theology. Dake held to a very literal interpretation of the Bible. Much of his attempts at interpreting Scripture did not even involve reading the Bible, as he claimed that the Holy Spirit taught him hundreds of verses without his ever having to read or memorize them. His *Dake's Annotated Reference Bible* taught racial segregation, and gave what he called *"30 Reasons for the Separation of the Races."* Those thirty reasons, comments based on Acts 17:26, are as follows:

DAKE'S ORIGINAL RACIST COMMENTS

"30 Reasons for the Separation of the Races Acts 17:26

1. God wills all races to be as He made them. Any violation of God's original purpose manifests insubordination to Him. (Acts 17:26, Rom. 9:19-24)

2. God made everything to reproduce "after his own kind" (Gen 1:11-12, 6:20, 7:14). Kind means type and color. He would have kept them all alike to begin with had he intended equality.
3. God originally determined the bounds of the habitations of nations, so they would be saved. (17:26, Gen.10:5,32, 11:8, Dt. 32:8)

4. Miscegenation means the mixture of the races, especially the black and white races, or those of outstanding type, or color. The Bible even goes farther than this. It is against different branches of the same stock intermarrying such as Jews marrying other descendants of Abraham (Ezra 9-10, Neh. 9-13, Jer 50:37, Ezek 30:5)

5. Abraham forbad Eliezer to take a wife for Isaac of Canaanites (Gen. 24:1-4). God was so pleased with this that He directed whom to get (Gen. 24:7, 12-67)

6. Isaac forbad Jacob to take a wife of the Canaanites (Gen. 27:46-28:7)

7. Abraham sent all his sons of the concubines, and even of his second wife, far away from Isaac so their descendants would not mix (Gen. 25:1-6)

8. Esau disobeying this law brought the final break between him and his father after lifelong companionship with him (Gen 25:28, 26:34-35, 27:46, 28:8-9)

9. The two branches of Isaac remained segregated forever (Gen 36, 46:8-26)

10. Ishmael and Isaac's descendants remained segregated forever (Gen 25:12-23, 1 Chr 1:29)

11. Jacobs's sons destroyed a whole city to maintain segregation (Gen 34)

12. God forbad intermarriage between Israel and all other nations (Ex 34:12-16, Dt 7:3-6)

13. Joshua forbad the same thing on sentence of death (Josh 23:12-13)

14. God cursed angels for leaving their own "first estate" and "their own habitation" to marry the daughters of men (Gen 6:1-4, 2 Pet 2:4, Jude 6,7)

15. Miscegenation caused Israel to be cursed (Judges 3:6-7, Num 25:1-8). Note that Phinehas' act was righteous (Ps 106:30)

16. This was Solomon's sin (1 King 11)

17. This was the sin of Jews returning from Babylon (Ezra 9:1-10:2, 10-18, 44, Neh. 13:1-30)

18. God commanded Israel to be segregated (Lev 20:24, Num 23:9, 1 King 8:53)

19. Jews recognized as a separate people in all ages because of God's choice and command (Matt 10:6, John 1:11). Equal rights in the gospel gives no right to break this eternal law

20. Segregation between Israelites and all other nations to remain in all eternity (Is 2:2-4,Ezek 37, 47:13-48, Zech 14:16-21, Matt 19:28, Lk 1:32-33, Rev 7:1-8, 14:1-5)

21. All nations will remain segregated from one another in their own parts of the earth forever (Acts 17:26, Gen 10:5, 32, 11:8-9, Dt 32:8, Dan 7:13-14, Rev 11:15, 21:24)

22. Certain people in Israel were not even to worship

with others (Dt 23:1-3, Ezra 10:8, Neh 9:2, 10:28, 13:3)

23. Even in heaven certain groups will not be allowed to worship together (Rev 7:7-17, 14:1-5, 15:2-5)

24. Segregation in the O.T. was so strong that an ox and an ass could not be worked together (Dt 22:10)

25. Miscegenation caused disunity among God's people (Num 12)

26. Stock was forbidden to be bred with other kinds (Lev 19:19)

27. Sowing mixed seed in the same field was unlawful (Lev 19:19)

28. Different seeds were forbidden to be planted in the same vineyards (Dt 22:9)

29. Wearing garments of mixed fabrics forbidden (Dt 22:11, Lev 19:19)

30. Christians and certain other people of a like race are to be segregated based upon behavior (Mt 18:15-17, 1 Cor 5:9-13, 6:15, 2 Cor 6:14-18, Eph 5:11, 2 Thess 3:6-16, 1 Tim 6:5, 2 Tim 3:5)"[21]

DAKE PUBLISHING PUT ON THE HOT SEAT BY DR. FREDERICK PRICE

After reading Dake's *30 Reasons* it was difficult for me to believe Dake Publishing's account that "In the 27 years between 1963 and 1990, only three people ever questioned us about the possibility of racial implications in some of the notes. In 1990, however, a few individuals did express concerns, especially to a list on page 159 of the New Testament, which was at that time titled "30 reasons for segregation of races."[22]

A position paper explaining the companies views on racism was written in response to a teaching series that was planned by Dr. Frederick K. C. Price, a popular television preacher and pastor of the Crenshaw Christian Center in Los Angeles. Dr. Price presented as series entitled "Race, Religion, and Racism," which consisted of over sixty weeks of lessons that sent shockwaves through the Christian Church in America. Rev. Price spent several years studying the issue and has published at least three volumes on the topic.

The end result of Dake's encounter with Dr. Price was what Dake Publishing described as a "unanimous decision to edit or remove any note that could possibly be misconstrued as a racist comment."[23] Although they made some revisions, the new version is simply the same old racist comments under a different heading. Let's take a look at Dake Publishing's weak attempt to remove their racist comments:

DAKE'S REVISED RACIST COMMENTS

"Separation in Scripture (17:26)

This verse says God made "all nations of men" from "one blood"; it also speaks of the "bounds of their habitation." In spite of a common ancestry from Adam first and later Noah, it was God's will for man to scatter over the earth, to "be fruitful and multiply" (Gen. 1:28; 8:17; 9:1). Man's failure to obey caused God to confuse his language (Gen. 11:1-9 and to physically separate the nations by dividing the earth into continents (Gen. 10:25). Both physically and spiritually, separation has been a consistent theme for God's people.

1   Separation for Messiah's line:

(1) Before and after Noah's flood, fallen angels (sons of God in Gen. 6:1-4) married human women and had giant offspring. This was done to corrupt the human race and prevent the birth of the Messiah, the Seed of the women prophesied in Gen. 3:15. See notes on **Giants After the Flood**, p. 94 of O.T.

(2) Destruction of the corrupt human race was the reason for the flood in Noah's day. See notes, Gen. 6

(3) God preserved Noah because he and his family were the only pure Adamites left. See note a, Gen. 6:9

(4) Satan continually tried to prevent Messiah's birth by corrupting Israel through intermarriage with Canaanites whose race included giant offspring. One reason for Israel's separation as a nation was to preserve their purity for the birth of the Messiah. See note j, Gen. 24:3

2   Separation in Israel:

(1) Abraham forbad Eliezer to take a Canaanite wife for Isaac (Gen. 24:1-4). God was pleased and He directed whom to get (Gen. 24:7-67)

(2) Isaac forbad Jacob to take a Canaanite wife (Gen. 27:46-28:7)

(3) Abraham sent the sons of his concubines and his second wife far away from Isaac so their descendants would not mix (Gen. 25:1-6)

(4) Esau's disobedience deeply grieved his parents (Gen 25:28; 26:34-35; 27:46; 28:8-9)

(5) Two branches of Isaac remain separate for ever (Gen. 36:46:8-26)

(6) Ishmael's and Isaac's descendants remain separate forever (Gen. 25:12-23; I Chr. 1:29)

(7) Jacob's sons destroyed a whole city to maintain separation (Gen. 34)

(8) God forbad Israel to intermarry (Ex. 34:12-16; Dt. 7:3-6)

(9) Intermarriage caused disunity among God's people (Num. 12)

(10) Enemies remained in the land as a penalty for this (Josh. 23:12-13)

(11) Intermarriage caused a curse on Israel (Judg. 3:6-7; Num. 25:1-8)

(12) This was Solomon's sin (1 Ki. 11)

(13) It was a sin of Jews returning from Babylon (Ezra 9; 10; Neh. 13)

(14) God told Israel to be separated (Lev. 20:24; Num. 23:9; 1 Ki. 8:53)

(15) Jews are recognized as a separate people in all ages because of God's choice (Mt. 10:6; Jn. 1:11)

(16) Separation between Jews and all other nations is to remain in eternity (Isa. 2:2-4; Ez. 37; 47:13-48; Zech. 14:16-21; Mt. 19:28; Lk. 1:32-33; Rev. 7:1-8; 14:1-5)

(17) Certain people in Israel were not to worship with others (Dt. 23:13; Ezra 10:8; Neh. 9:2; 10:28; 13:3)

3 Miscellaneous separation:

(1) An ox and an ass could not be worked together (Dt. 22:10)

(2) Stock was forbidden to be bred with other kinds (Lev. 19:19)

(3) Sowing mixed seed in the same field was unlawful (Lev. 19:19)

(4) Different seeds were forbidden to be planted in vineyards (Dt. 22:9)

(5) Wearing garments of mixed fabrics forbidden (Dt. 22:11; Lev. 19:19)

4 <u>Christian separation:</u> Christians to be separate from certain people at times (Mt. 18:15-17; 1 Cor. 5:9-13; 6:15; 2 Cor. 6:14-18; 2 Th. 3:6, 14; 1 Tim. 6:5; 2 Tim. 3:5)"[24]

WHERE ARE THE CHANGES?

As you can see, all of the 30 Reasons for the Separation of the Races are contained in the notes contained in the "revised version." This brings up an interesting question. What was the purpose of Dake's "position paper" when they obviously had no real intention to remove the racist comments, which they have printed for so many years? Let's take a look at their position paper in its entirety:

"Answering the Charge of Racism
A Position Paper From Dake Publishing

A Brief History of the Problem

Since it was first published in its entirety in 1963, *The Dake Annotated Reference Bible* has been enjoyed by hundreds of thousands of people from every nationality, every denomination, and all walks of life. The depth of its teachings and the insight it gave into the Scriptures all bore witness to the gifting and character of its author, Finis Jennings Dake.

Dake Bible Sales, the publishing company started by Finis and Dorothy Dake, is now known as Dake Publishing, Inc. We are a small company that remains family-owned and operated to this day.

In the 27 years between 1963 and 1990, only three people ever questioned us about the possibility of racial implications in some of the notes. In 1990, however, a few individuals did express concerns, especially to a list on page 159 of the New Testament which was at that time titled "30 reasons for segregation of races."

But Finis Dake had only been dead since 1987, and we were more than a little hesitant to make any significant changes to his work. We felt it our responsibility, both as his family and his publishers, to preserve Dake's teachings in their entirety. We saw the evidence of God's favor in the enduring quality of his work, especially in *The Dake Annotated Reference Bible*. Nevertheless, when this note on page 159 was brought to our attention from the perspective of those who were offended by what they thought was racism, we began immediately to address the issue.

Having grown up (literally) under his ministry, we understood Dake's teachings. We knew that Finis Dake was not a racist. Therefore, we were concerned at first only with the wording of the notes. We started by substituting "separation" for the more racially charged "segregation" throughout the Dake Bible. (This was done even though context proves that

Dake's broad use of the term usually referred to such things as God's command that Israel be a separate people.) We also used "nation" instead of "race" where it offered clarity, and we updated a few other words that were common in Dake's day, but offensive in our own.

But as we moved further into the 1990s, more negative reactions to such notes began to surface, and we realized that certain notes were a stumbling block for some whose hearts were already wounded from their experiences of racial prejudice. They simply couldn't move past this stumbling block to see what Dake was really saying. And so, in the fall of 1996, we discussed the matter as a family and made a unanimous decision to edit or remove any note that could possibly be misconstrued as a racist comment. The first printing to reflect these changes was done in January of 1997.

Enter Dr. Frederick K. C. Price

In spite of these efforts on our part, on February 16, 1998, Dake Publishing learned that Dr. Frederick K. C. Price intended to devote at least 30 weeks of his series on "Race, Religion, and Racism" to the original notes on page 159 of the New Testament.

As we sought the Lord and godly counsel, we concluded that God would have us to approach Dr. Price in humility. This is the text of our letter to him on February 18, 1998:

Dr. Frederick K. C. Price:

We are writing this letter to you personally, to your congregation, and to your television audience. We wish to express our sincere regrets and apologies for any commentary in *The Dake Annotated Reference Bible* that has been interpreted as being supportive of slavery, racism or discrimination. Neither Finis Dake nor any member of the Dake family would ever want to contribute to the oppression of African-Americans or any other race of people.

As a new convert, Finis Dake often attended a Black church and was baptized there. He frequently preached in Black churches throughout the country, and Blacks attended the churches that he pastored as well. He held in the highest esteem his many African-American brothers who dedicated their lives to the ministry of the Gospel and the full experience of the Holy Spirit. Further more, we know that people of color throughout the world have played a vital role in winning many souls to Christ, though most of them have not been publicly recognized.

Dr. Dake was neither a racist, nor proud. In fact, in the early 1930s he wrote a booklet entitled *One Hundred Fifty Jawbreakers for Anglo-Saxons*, refuting the Anglo-Saxon theory which supports the notion of white supremacy. This publication is inconsistent with the idea that his reference notes on racial separation were intended to advocate white

91

supremacy. In addition, his notes on Colossians 3:11-12 clearly state that "as a new creation in Christ there is no distinction made in rights and privileges because of race, sex, color, or position in life."

From our hearts, we are certain that Dr. Dake never intended for his reference notes to be used to support racism of any kind. Yet we clearly see how his thirty reasons for the separation of the nations can be interpreted as advocating racism, and we agree that racism has no place in the body of Christ, or anywhere else. Please accept this letter as a public statement from the entire Dake family that we ask for forgiveness.

Dr. Dake's reference notes were based on his understanding of the Word of God. However, we do not wish the Dake notes to offend anyone through confusion about this sensitive topic. Therefore, we have labored to omit all racially insensitive references. We have enclosed a new Dake Bible, printed in January of 1997, for your use. We hope you will agree that the changes it contains demonstrate our commitment to reach out with an open heart to help heal the pains of racial injustice. The Dake Bible has blessed hundreds of thousands of people all over the world, and we want it to continue to promote spiritual growth, healing and reconciliation.

You mentioned in your sermon last Sunday that radiation treatments to cure cancer, if not administered properly, can be just as deadly as the cancer itself. The Dake family agrees that racial prejudice in the body of Christ is, and has been, a cancerous schism to our fellowship and a hindrance to the witness of His name. However, like the radiation treatments you mentioned, the public airing of these problems could be just as dangerous as the evil of racism itself.

Therefore, we ask that you would consider meeting with us and with other Christian leaders so that we can seek to resolve these issues in ways that will be of the greatest benefit to the body of Christ, to our ministries, and to the thousands and even millions of souls who can come to the Lord once they see that we are truly united in love as our Lord commanded.

We have gone to great lengths to change the Dake notes so that they will not offend any ethnic or racial group. We will go to even greater lengths to have full reconciliation and forgiveness between ourselves and our Christian brothers and sisters, regarding this issue. We feel confident that you will join us in this endeavor. Therefore, we wait to hear from you as soon as possible, so that the details of such a conference can be arranged.

Dr. Price, none of us can undo our personal, familial, or national histories. But we can direct the present and the future. As you seek God's direction in the weeks to come, we urge you to prayerfully consider this letter as a public appeal for forgiveness and healing. You are in a position to speak life or death, to build up or destroy, to extend mercy or withhold it.

Your humble servants,
Finis Dake Jr.
Annabeth Dake Germaine
Finette Dake Kennedy
Derrick Germaine

In this letter we humbled ourselves before Dr. Price, as much as we knew how. This was not feigned humility, but genuine. It was motivated in part by our desire to be sensitive to an offended brother. It also reflected our hearts as we endeavor to conduct ourselves as servants of Christ. And it was certainly our hope that his heart would be softened, and that he might reconsider his plans to include the Dake Bible in his series on "Race, Religion, and Racism."

However, on February 25, we received a response from Dr. Price:

To the Dake Family:

Greetings in the wonderful name of Jesus.

In response to your faxed letter dated February 18, 1998, I must say, I was surprised to say the least, to have received a letter from you. I don't know what I've done to deserve this honor.

It is true that I am in the process of teaching a series on "Race, Religion and Racism", in my church and ultimately to the body of Christ at large. God gave me this assignment about seven years ago. For the last three years I have been doing extensive research on the subject. We have a horrendous problem of racism in the church; which no one else seems to want to address in depth. This is my task. In order to destroy racism in the church, we must locate its roots and pull them out of the ground of the heart of the church. It is a fact that must be admitted that White Christians (people) **not all**, but far too many, hold negative attitudes and opinions about African-Americans. Where do attitudes and opinions come from? From observation, association and teaching. Racial and color prejudice (racism) is not genetically transmitted, nor is it passed through the blood. It is socially transmitted from father to son, from father to son and on and on it goes. The major transmitters of racism have been the teachings in the home by parents and teachings in the church by religious leaders, both preachers and teachers, both from the pulpit and the printed page.

The Lord has led me to go back to the past and pull up the roots that have produced the present! I have never said nor inferred that Dr. Dake was a racist. After all, I have never met him. I operate on the basis of two Biblical principles among many others, which state in Matthew 12:33 "Either make the tree good, and His fruit good; or else make the tree corrupt and His fruit corrupt; for the tree is known by His fruit." And 1 Thessalonians 5:22, "Abstain from all appearance of evil." No human is omniscient enough to know what is in the heart or mind of another human, until they speak, write or act. Based upon that, the Holy Spirit has led me to research volumes of material, both secular and Christian, to find the roots of racism and dig them up....

Do you have any idea of how many people have bought and studied the Dake Bible from 1963-1998 **(35 years)**?. People who have these Bibles must be informed that these particular notes must be discarded.

In your letter you mentioned, "We wish to express our sincere regrets and apologies for any commentary in The Dake Annotated Reference Bible that has been interpreted as being supportive of slavery, racism or discrimination." To me this issue is not personal, however, I for one would be the first to say to you, apologies accepted! But, the fact of the matter still stands, the notes are already printed and have been circulating for the past 35 years. It has to be fixed! I see two ways by which this can possibly be done. First, when automobile manufacturers, Ford, General Motors etc. find a flaw in their product, they do a recall at their expense. In other words, they fix or replace the faulty part; are you willing to do that? Thirty-five years of printed material ...that's a lot of "parts". Secondly, someone has to point out the faulty parts, so people can avoid them. That is a part of my assignment with this series on "Race, Religion, and Racism"....

Thank you for writing and for your concern (it is my concern also) for the Body of Christ.

In the service of the King,

Frederick K. C. Price, Ph.D.

The following Sunday, March 1, 1998, Dr. Price read both letters to his congregation. But he primed his congregation the week before, saying,

> "They put a letter on me, in fact, it almost...appears that they want to put a guilt trip on me. But see, they don't realize that *God* gave me this assignment some years back. I've done the research on this series for three years, a straight three years."

He then took what we intended to be a move toward healing and used it instead to add fuel to the fire. As he stated in his letter to us, he feels it is his "assignment" to "point out the faulty parts" in older printings of the Dake Bible. This he plans to do for weeks to come.

We wrote a second letter to Dr. Price, stressing again our desire to meet with him, both to hear his concerns and, hopefully, to clarify matters. In his reply, however, he said he would prefer that we wait until he was finished with his series, so that we could fully understand his perspective. But after listening to several subsequent messages, his perspective became quite obvious. Sickened by what we heard, we've chosen not to respond to Dr. Price any further. Instead, we feel it necessary to issue this position paper stating clearly and accurately the truth about the so-called "racism" in the Dake Bible.

Dake's Perspective

At this point, we would like to clarify Dake's use of "white" with regard to race. Finis Dake understood this word in a much broader sense than the "snow white" or "European white" understanding Dr. Price has ascribed to the term in some of his recent messages. Dake's usage of "white" was consistent with the dictionary explanation that there are only three main ethnic divisions of the human race--Caucasian (white), Negroid (black) and Mongoloid (oriental).

We do not know all of the sources Dake relied upon while doing his research. But we do know that he kept a tattered copy of *Webster's Unabridged Dictionary* nearby. According to *Webster's New Universal Unabridged Dictionary* (Deluxe Second Edition, ©1983), the Caucasian division is composed not only of "whites" (which is loosely synonymous with Caucasian and embraces the Alpine and Nordic subdivisions), but also includes all people of Mediterranean descent. *Webster's New World Dictionary* (© 1976) further qualifies the term as including "peoples of Europe, North Africa, the Near East, India, etc. and is loosely called the *white race* although it embraces peoples of dark skin color." In addition, the 1958 *Britannica World Language Dictionary* (which Dake referred to often) states that Caucasian pertains to "peoples speaking Indo-European, Semitic, Hamitic languages." The same dictionary, under the heading of **race**, states that "according to some authorities, the primary stocks

98

are: the Caucasian (Nordic, Alpine, Mediterranean, and Hindu), the Mongoloid (Mongolian, Malaysian, and American Indian), and the Negroid (Negro, Negrito, and Melanesian)."

Basically, according to this understanding, a Caucasian is anyone who isn't Negroid or Mongoloid. And since Caucasian is loosely synonymous with "white" (although modern racial sensitivity has led us to refrain from such usage), Dake was not out of line to write this way in his day.

Had the primary figures in the Bible fallen into any other ethnic division, Dake would have had no problem noting that. Finis Dake didn't care what color Jesus or any other biblical character was. He didn't associate them with Caucasians because of some personal agenda to identify the major figures of the Bible with the white race; he did so because they were already grouped that way, in his understanding.

Granted, it would have been helpful for him to have qualified his use of such terminology, especially for readers today. But it never occurred to him that he would later be accused of being a racist or a white supremacist. (Perhaps a rough parallel exists between the intentions of the founders of our Constitution and the often-absurd interpretations their words are given today.)

Finis Dake only made references to such matters because of his understanding from the Bible that God divided the nations after the incident with the tower of Babel. His literal interpretation of Scripture (including such statements as "the bounds of their habitation" in Acts 17:26) led him to conclude that God intended the human race to remain divided in this way. This was not a view resulting from racial prejudice, but from his very literal biblical exegesis.

Dr. Price has emphasized Rev. Dake's usage of racial distinctions, particularly in reference to a note entitled *Separation in Scripture*. Point number four states that "Miscegenation means the mixture of races, especially the black and white races, or those of outstanding type or color." Dr. Price sees racism in the phrase "especially the black and white races," and has spent a great deal of time trying to prove his point.

However, here again we have a very clear example of Finis Dake's use of common definitions to clearly illustrate a point. This phrase is taken from Webster's Unabridged Dictionary, which defines miscegenation as "marriage or interbreeding between members of different races, especially in the United States, between whites and Negroes." Again, Funk and Wagnall's New Practical Standard Dictionary defines miscegenation as "interbreeding of races, especially intermarriage or interbreeding between white and Negro, or white and Oriental races."

Far from being an example of racism, this is merely an example of Finis Dake's use of contemporary reference materials to clarify a statement.

Our Understanding of Racism

When we speak of racism, we do so according to its definition *in Webster's New Universal Unabridged Dictionary*: "a doctrine or feeling of racial differences or antagonisms, especially with reference to supposed racial superiority, inferiority, or purity; racial prejudice." The same dictionary defines prejudice as (1), "a judgment or opinion formed before the facts are known; preconceived idea, favorable or, more usually, unfavorable"; (2), "a judgment or opinion held in disregard of facts that contradict it"; (3), "the holding of such judgments or opinions"; and (4), "suspicion, intolerance, or hatred of other races, creeds, religions, occupations, etc."

In short, as we understand it, the key components of racism are a sense of superiority of one race over another, and prejudice--a pre-judgment against someone because of their race.

Dr. Price has mentioned his "acid test" of racism (which seems to focus primarily on one's attitude toward interracial marriage); this is ours: to be guilty of racism, there must be an undeniable assertion of the superiority of one race over another, and a prejudicial bias against those of a race different from one's own. Every printing of the Dake Bible is free of racism, according to this simple test.

Dr. Price has made repeated and emphatic reference to the **appearance** of racism in the Dake Bible. To the contrary, we assert that *no* statement in *any* printing of the Dake Bible is guilty of racism or prejudice, by these commonly understood definitions. No matter how strongly someone disagrees with any statement in the Dake Bible, one will never find anything in it that even hints at the superiority of whites over blacks or any other race. Such motivation can only be read into the text from the outside. At best (or at worst, depending on your perspective), the reader is left only with his or her own speculation as to Dake's intentions for writing what he did. In other words, even the **appearance** of racism will disappear when one takes the time to separate what was actually written from one's own preconceived ideas of the author's motivations.

This is not to say that we care nothing for the feelings of those who are offended when they read Dake's notes. On the contrary, it is for this very reason that we made the changes in the 1997 printing. We did not make these changes because the Dake Bible was full of racist commentary. We made the changes because we had no desire to offend those who had suffered so long from racial injustice that they could not help but see evidences of racism--even where none existed.

Wounded in the House of Our Friends

The commentary notes in the Dake Bible contain nearly half again as much text as the Scriptures themselves. No one could write so extensively and so forthrightly about so many topics and expect to escape criticism. It's not criticism of the Dake Bible that has hurt us over the years. It's the sense of betrayal by people we thought were our brothers and sisters in the Lord that has left the most painful and lasting wounds. In Zechariah's prophetic portrayal of Christ, such wounds are "those with which I was wounded in the house of my friends" (Zech. 13:6).

One brother misrepresented the Dake Bible repeatedly before conference audiences in excess of 50,000. Another spoke his mind (but not the truth) on several broadcasts of a national Christian radio program. And more than one prominent Christian magazine has run articles that were ruinously unfair and damaging. But not once in our history has anyone ever come to us first. Not once has any of our critics expressed their concerns to us privately before airing them publicly.

Enter Charisma

Charisma's recent article (in the April, 1998 issue) is a case in point. They were already doing a piece on Fred Price and Kenneth Hagin, Jr. When they learned of our letter to Price, they wanted to include a portion of it in an article.

We were thrilled by this turn of events and provided an edited version of our letter within the hour. But because we've been misrepresented in the past, we asked to read the article before it went to press. We were told this was not their policy. We stated strongly that we didn't even want it in print if it was going to be a negative piece for Dake.

When the article came out in print, it bore the shocking headline: DAKE PUBLISHING APOLOGIZES FOR RACIST REMARKS IN BIBLE.

And instead of containing our letter, it was a story about our company, Finis Dake, and the Dake Bible. A grand total of three sentences from our letter closed the piece.

Many of our shocked customers read the article before we did. Some were outraged at the way we'd been misrepresented (again). Others expressed concern about their Dake Bibles, once they had read the article. **"It's Not Personal, It's Principle."**

But the most appalling abuse we've received has been from Dr. Frederick K. C. Price. He claims repeatedly that his attacks on the Dake Bible aren't personal, but are a matter of principle. Yet his own actions toward us exhibit a disturbing lack of such principle.

Jesus taught that if our brother sins against us, we should confront him privately:

> "Moreover if thy brother shall trespass against thee, go and tell him his fault between thee and him alone: if he shall hear thee, thou hast gained thy brother. But if he will not hear thee, then take with thee one or two more, that in the mouth of two or three witnesses every word may be established. And if he shall neglect to hear them, tell it unto the church: but if he neglect to hear the church, let him be unto thee as an heathen man and a publican" (Mt. 18: 15-17, KJV).

We aren't to "tell it unto the church" (as Dr. Price is doing) until we've taken one or two others to confront him again, "that in the mouth of two or three witnesses every word may be established."

Since Dr. Price evidently believes the Dake Bible is guilty of the sin of racism, he should have come to us privately as our brother in Christ. But this he did not do. In fact, he doesn't want to meet with us until he finishes his series. By then, though, the damage will have been done. He will have spent many weeks trying to destroy the credibility of the Dake Bible on national television, when it could all be avoided if he would just sit down and talk with us as our brother in Christ. Looking at it this way, it is impossible to swallow his claim that "it's not personal."

As was stated at the beginning of this paper, we've been working to remove the perception of racism in the Dake Bible since 1990. (We can't remove actual racism, because there isn't any.) As this activity progressed, we felt it wise to solicit the perspective of someone outside of the Dake family, and we felt that Dr. Price would be the ideal candidate. Finis Dake, Jr. spoke to Dr. Price on the phone and followed up with a letter to him on April 29, 1994, inviting him to comment on any portion of the Dake notes that even hinted of racism--including the "30 reasons" on page 159 of the New Testament. Dr. Price never responded to us. Yet he stated in his letter to us on February 25, 1998, that God gave him this assignment "about seven years ago." And in his recent tapes he says that he has been researching this subject diligently for the last three years. Furthermore, the Dake Bible he quotes from was printed in 1971, so Dake's teachings aren't a recent discovery for him.

How is it possible that Dr. Price had nothing to say when we welcomed his suggestions four years ago, but now he feels it's his God-given duty to air his criticisms on television, before an audience of millions? He reminds his audience repeatedly that he's dealing with principles, with right and wrong. To our knowledge, there is not a single Scriptural principle which justifies this behavior on his part. It is just plain wrong.

105

Conclusion

We love Dr. Price and respect the obvious anointing he has had in times past. And we continue to pray for God's blessings on him, his family, and his ministry. Like David, we do not wish to touch the Lord's anointed and so bring judgment upon ourselves. The battle is the Lord's.

Still, we feel a responsibility as the publishers of *The Dake Annotated Reference Bible* to clarify our official position on this issue. It is our hope and prayer that those who have been offended by portions of the Dake Bible in the past will now see more clearly both Dake's heart and our own. And for those who believe we've compromised somehow in the changes we've made, we hope the necessity for such changes is now evident.

However, it is on this one issue alone that we feel changing the Dake Bible was for the greater good of the body of Christ. The remainder of Dake's extensive teachings will be preserved. There is no question in our minds that God anointed Finis Jennings Dake to teach the Word, and to record those teachings in The Dake Annotated Reference Bible and his other great works. His wording wasn't always perfect, but he definitely had an anointing.

With this fact always in mind, it is the ongoing commitment of Dake Publishing to handle the writings of Finis Jennings Dake with both care, honor and humility.

David Patton, editor

Dake Publishing, Inc.

May, 1998"

THE BOTTOM LINE ABOUT
THE WRITINGS OF FINIS DAKE

I have never seen a more ridiculous explanation to justify years of spreading blatant racism. What is even more appalling is the audacity of Dake Publishing to attack Dr. Price for challenging the racist ideology that they have supported and spread for generations. The fact that they continue to publish the same racist notes speaks volumes about their sincerity.

The racism expressed by Finis Jennings Dake, that God wills for races be kept separate in terms of family, national boundaries or social and economic development, is no different than what was practiced in racist South Africa during the apartheid era.

The citation of Acts 17:26 by Dake is typical in the literature of racist theologians. However, the text means nothing in terms of racism, and says nothing about racial intermarriage or the setting up of apartheid-like policies. It is simply Paul's attempt to appeal to the philosophical system of his hearers. Paul can hardly be held up as a poster child for racial separation. He was the one who had opposed Peter "to his face" for his failure to mix with the non-Jewish Christians (Galatians 2:11-14).

Notwithstanding much Scriptural evidence, racist separatist use the misinterpretation of Acts 17:26 and other ideas in an effort to prove that intermarriage and racial interaction is anti-Christian.

107

Dake's reasoning is similar to that of the Knights of the Ku Klux Klan. Their race ideology is based upon the United States being a Christian nation. Based on this, they believe that the advancement of white people means separate development and existence of different races. The critical observer will agree that Dake's racist theology does not derive its doctrines from an impartial reading of its sources. As a matter of fact, it is probably wrong to call what Dake has to say on the matter of race a theology. His writings are more of a predetermined ideology. His ideology, though using the power of religion and religious language, does not originate within a religious context, but a social and political context that uses religion for its own purposes.

One may ask why racists use religion to further their agenda. It is quite simple; religion dominates all parts of a person's life. The genuinely religious person will base most of life's decisions concerning morality, work and economy, law, education, marriage, family and community life on religious beliefs.

Religion is potent at controlling people's actions. It is no wonder Karl Marx regarded religion as the opium of the masses. Religion can and does have great power over the lives of individuals and communities. That power can have a dangerous effect in keeping oppressed people passive and subservient.

FURTHERING RACIST CAUSES

I in no wise am making a judgment on Finis Dake or any other so-called theologian as I am well aware that well-intentioned people can stumble into an unintentional forms of racism. Often, non-racist Christians can further the racist cause, even if they do so inadvertently. However, it is imperative that Christians discard racist ideologies once they are exposed.

What Dake Publishing obviously has trouble coming to grips with is the fact that Finis Dake held racist views and they are guilty of spreading his racist ideology throughout the Christian world. True humility would result in a sincere apology for the hurt caused by Dake's writings and the immediate removal of the comments from their publications. Anything less is unacceptable and sinful.

CHAPTER 8

CONCLUSION

The relationship between racism and religion run far back into the evolutionary past. Sadly, the most thorough practice of racism during the last thousand years or so has involved Christians. Christianity has become the emblem of the teaching of racial supremacy.

The most virulent forms of racism in America today all involve religious organizations. In addition to the "Christian Knights of the Ku Klux Klan," there is the so-called Christian Identity movement, which preaches hatred of Blacks and Jews, an imminent apocalypse, and the propriety of using armed violence to achieve its goals. The movement includes individual organizations with names such as "Church of Jesus Christ Christian," "Aryan Nations," "The Order," "The Covenant," and "the Sword and the Arm of the Lord." Even though civilization is now nearly five thousand years old, many of the world's religions dangerously continue to reinforce erroneous theories of racial inequality.

American racism is blatant, subtle and conveniently concealed behind a syndrome that denies its reality. Racism is an idolatrous self-worship, it is a violation of God's intent that there should be no distinctions made concerning race. Racism is deeply entrenched in the fabric and psyche of the American religious landscape.

In our time the religious landscape reflects the class, gender, and racial polarization that is so predominant in our society. The Christian church has failed to collectively and prophetically indict racism in word and deed. When pastors and evangelists, both Black and white, begin to address racism with the same fervor that they preach on faith and healing, a major change will take place. Repentance is the key and only road to racial liberation and reconciliation.

While it cannot be denied that the church is set amid racial tensions, the fact that there are racial tensions in the church is often ignored. It is extremely naïve to think that persons who hold racial prejudice in their hearts have released those feelings by simply joining a church. Most Christians believe that a confession of faith as described in Romans 10 is the final step in the salvation process. Contrary to that belief, it is the first step on a long journey to becoming truly converted. Racial tensions among those in the church are the evidence of unregenerateness. Church members do not like the thought that it may be their own unconvertedness or their own unregenerateness that causes racial tension within the church. Therefore it becomes easy for those unwilling to face this reality to think it possible that God approves of racial discrimination, that it is part of his creative plan. Then there are those who choose to think that although God does not like racial tension, he knows how inevitable it is, and therefore his divine plan is that the races ought to stay away from one another. The church has failed to challenge racist laws and to stand against a whole array of regulations, social arrangements, customs, and traditions that promote the superiority of one race over another.

Too many in the church convince themselves that they personally have no race prejudice, yet, when considering local customs and local prejudices they do little to change the status quo. Many accept racial equality in theory, but accept racial inequality in practice.

THE CHURCH'S DENIAL OF RACISM

The denial of the reality of racism by the church is a serious problem. Dave Claerbaut, a White urban missionary, makes a rather telling point about the source of racism and asserts that it is not meant to be an indictment. He states: ". . .to be white and somewhat racist is normal. For just as a person who regularly breathes polluted city air should not be the least defensive about having some pollution in his lungs, so a person who is regularly exposed to a racist and prejudice-laden society could hardly be expected not to be somewhat prejudiced. . . .if white racism is defined as having notions of white supremacy, it becomes rather easy to see how these tendencies become subconsciously internalized at a very early age. Thus, these racist notions calcify. All agree that a person's environment is a major influence on his attitudes, values, beliefs and behaviors. Thus, a white pastor or urban worker is by conditioning and environment at least partly racist."[25]

In spite of Claerbaut's analysis, implicit in the Christian Church at large, is a colossal effort to deny racism's existence. Many church leaders often downplay the existence, gravity, or significance of acts of bias. Suspect phrases include: "It's an isolated incident," "You're making a mountain out of a molehill," "She didn't mean anything by that," and "We won't get anywhere by dwelling on the past." The history of racism along with any current racist acts or statements, left unchallenged, sends the wrong message to people everywhere. It is unproductive to simply dismiss any attempt by Blacks to challenge racism as an act of "playing the race card." After all, if whites had not placed the card in the deck it could never be played.

Christians must admit that church's history with respect to the treatment of non-white people is not something in which it can take pride. Attitudes of racial and cultural superiority have led to a suppression of non-white culture and values. There must be recognition of the impact of these actions. The church must acknowledge that the result of its actions was the erosion of the political, economic and social standing of people of color. In America, with the complicity of the church, people of color face institutionalized racism, which concentrates poverty and disadvantage in their communities and often denies them opportunities for meaningful participation in American public life.

The church must come to grips with its record of racism. It is unpleasant for those who lay claim to a relationship with Jesus Christ to think of themselves as unregenerate. This attitude is intensely human, but is not noble, courageous or generous. The church's attitude toward its prejudice has been cautious, calculating and cold. It seems as though, in large part, the church has ruled out any possibility that God may be calling them to transcend differences of race and culture and calling them to assert Christian unity in a race-ridden world.

The church as a whole is not concerned enough about its conformity to this country's culture of racism, prejudice, and discrimination. It is easy to condemn the results of these evils, but it is the evil itself that needs the church's condemnation. The best way for the church to condemn the color bar is to show that it does not have one.

Christians must seek for a sincere, visible unity of all Christians. I remain unimpressed by arguments for a spiritual unity that are not followed by sincere, visible expression. Christians must show their unity to the world; it is the only true witness that our Lord is truly the hope of the world.

The story of racial unity and division as it has been portrayed within American history is not a very happy one. In a very real sense and to a great extent, the church has lost its prophetic promise, the ability to provide a viable model in which disparate races dwell together in harmony as the reconciled people of God. This has happened due to fear of the unknown, coupled with a capitulation to contemporary culture. We have, in fact, "conformed to the world."

A STRATEGY FOR RACIAL HARMONY

I would like to conclude by offering some suggestions toward a future strategy for racial harmony.

First, there must be an acknowledgement of past failures. There needs to be an acknowledgement that many of the white Christian pioneers failed to exercise prophetic leadership by not capitalizing on the opportunity for sustained racial reconciliation.

Second, Christians must move meaningfully toward the goal of unity that our Lord envisioned and commanded for the members of His Body, and which characterized those in the Upper Room (Acts 2:1-4). In order to do this there needs to be the convening of regular ecumenical, interdenominational, and cross-cultural gatherings that embrace people of diverse streams.

Third, there must also be the presence of an open and honest dialogue characterized by unbridled candor, possibly bordering on the brutal. Such candor would acknowledge the responsibility for the institutionalization of racial segregation within American society.

American Christians have missed a golden opportunity to allow the dynamic force of the Holy Spirit--which they believed could effect other wondrous and miraculous deeds--to countermand the sinful effects of an evil and unjust social order, they must, in all haste, make up for lost time. To continue

115

to deny the fact that white Christians encouraged, gladly welcomed, and even defended the culture of racism with all its invidious practices and to refuse to accept responsibility for such developments will only widen and prolongs distrust and estrangement.

The time is past for judging people on the basis of race. We are all members of the same endangered species, the human race, and we must all make accommodation for each other in various ways. We must judge people as individuals, not as members of one or another race.

While certain differences are likely to persist, Blacks and whites must continue to discuss the reasons for the deep chasm that divides them. It is only through open and honest dialogue and the acknowledgement of past failures can the church help to foster the kind of nation that Rev. Dr. Martin Luther King, Jr. spoke about in his famous "I Have a Dream" speech. Everyone desires to "live in a nation where they will not be judged by the color of their skin but by the content of their character."[26]

NOTES

[1] The History of the Negro Church, Carter G. Woodson, Ph.D. The Associated Publishers, Washington D.C., 1921, Second Edition, p. 28.

[2] The Black Church in the African American Experience, Lincoln and Mamiya, p. 8.

[3] Raboteau, Albert J. *African American Religion.* New York: Oxford University Press, 1999, p. 83

[4] Ibid

[5] Turner, Nat in *The Confessions of Nat Turner* by Thomas R. Gray, Baltimore: Thomas R. Gray, 1831, p. 338

[6] Ibid, p. 391

[7] Barndt, Joseph R. *Dismantling Racism.* Minneapolis: Augsburg Fortress, 1991.

[8] Jefferson, Thomas. "Notes on the State of Virginia." Philadelphia, 1801, 322.

[9] Knowles, Louis L. & Prewitt, Kenneth. *Institutional Racism in America.* Englewood Cliffs: Prentice-Hall Inc, 1969.

[10] Nida, Eugene A. *Customs and Cultures.* Pasadena: William Carey Library, 1954.

[11] Ibid

[12] Mathews, Donald G. *Religion in the Old South.* Chicago: The University of Chicago Press, 1977.

13   Barndt, Joseph R. *Dismantling Racism.* Minneapolis: Augsburg Fortress, 1991.

14 Banks, William L. *The Black Church in the United States.* Chicago: Moody Press, 1972.

15   Barndt, Joseph R. *Dismantling Racism.* Minneapolis: Augsburg Fortress, 1991.

16   Barndt, Joseph R. *Dismantling Racism.* Minneapolis: Augsburg Fortress, 1991.

17 Ibid

18 Thompson Jr., J. Earl. "The Return of the Racist Religion of the Republic." in, Smith, Elwyn A. Ed. *The Religion and the Republic.* Philadelphia: Fortress Press, 1971.

19 McKissick Sr., William Dwight. *Beyond Roots: In Search of Blacks in the Bible.* Wenonah, NJ: Renaissance Productions, 1990.

20   Latourette, Kenneth Scott. *A History of the Expansion of Christianity: Volume 1, The First Five Centuries.* Grand Rapids, MI: Zondervan Publishing House, 1970.

21 Dake, Finis J., ed. Dake Annotated Reference Bible. Lawrenceville, GA: Dake Publishing, Inc.., 1989.

22 Dake Publishing, Inc. *Answering the Charge of Racism: A Position Paper From Dake Publishing.* Lawrenceville, GA: Dake Publishing, Inc.

[23] Ibid.

[24] Dake, Finis J., ed. Dake Annotated Reference Bible. Lawrenceville, GA: Dake Publishing, Inc.., 1999.

[25] Claerbaut, David, *Urban Ministry*, (Grand Rapids, Michigan: Zondervan, 1983), 130.

[26] King, Martin Luther, Jr., *I Have a Dream,* Speech delivered on the steps at the Lincoln Memorial in Washington D.C. on August 28, 1963.

Made in the USA
Charleston, SC
29 February 2012